Small Woodworking
Shops

Small Woodworking Shops

The Editors of
Fine Woodworking

The Taunton Press

The Taunton Press, Inc., 63 South Main Street, PO Box 5506, Newtown, CT 06470-5506
e-mail: tp@taunton.com

Distributed by Publishers Group West

Jacket/Cover design: Susan Fazekas
Interior design and layout: Susan Fazekas

Cover Photographers: (front cover) Michael Pekovich, courtesy *Fine Woodworking,* © The Taunton Press, Inc.; (back cover, clockwise from upper left) Jonathan Binzen, courtesy *Fine Woodworking,* © The Taunton Press, Inc.; Jonathan Binzen, courtesy *Fine Woodworking,* © The Taunton Press, Inc.; Joe Tracy, courtesy *Fine Woodworking,* © The Taunton Press, Inc.

Fine Woodworking® is a trademark of The Taunton Press, Inc., registered in the U.S. Patent and Trademark Office.

Library of Congress Cataloging-in-Publication Data

Small woodworking shops : the new best of Fine woodworking / editors of
Fine woodworking.
      p. cm.
Includes index.
  ISBN 1-56158-686-2 paperback
  ISBN 1-56158-750-8 hardcover

 1. Workshops--Design and construction. 2. Workshops--Equipment and
supplies. 3. Woodworking tools. I. Fine woodworking.
TT152 .S635 2004
684'.04--dc22

                                        2003018325

Printed in the United States of America
10 9 8 7 6 5 4 3 2 1

Small Woodworking Shops was originally published in paperback in 2004 by The Taunton Press, Inc.

The following manufacturers/names appearing in *Small Woodworking Shops* are trademarks: Aearo®, AmericanAirFilter™, B-Line Systems Inc.®, Bench Dog Tools®, Betadine®, Biesemeyer®, Brainerd Manufacturing Co.®, Delta®, Donald Duck®, Duluth Trading Company®, Econ-o-watt®, Empire Comfort Systems®, General Electric®, Hepa®, Lee-son®, Leightning®, Lexan®, Lufkin®, Oneida®, Osram®, Peg-Board®, Peltor®, Philips®, Plexiglas®, Powermatic®, Pro Ears®, Quick-Fit™, SECO™, Starrett®, Supersaver®, Sylvania®, Tempwood®, The Pink Panther®, Veritas®, Watt-miser®

Working wood is inherently dangerous. Using hand or power tools improperly or ignoring safety practices can lead to permanent injury or even death. Don't try to perform operations you learn about here (or elsewhere) unless you're certain they are safe for you. If something about an operation doesn't feel right, don't do it. Look for another way. We want you to enjoy the craft, so please keep safety foremost in your mind whenever you're in the shop.

Acknowledgments

Special thanks to the authors, editors,
art directors, copy editors, and other
staff members of *Fine Woodworking* who
contributed to the development of the
articles in this book.

Contents

Introduction

Fortunate is the woodworker who can say his workshop is not wanting for more floor space. Most one-person shops, whether you work wood for recreation or vocation, are busting at the seams with lumber, scraps, tools, jigs and all the miscellaneous stuff that woodworkers collect in the course of building furniture. To make things worse, many of us put up with the ignominy of having to share our workspace with a washer and dryer or family car.

I've squeezed my woodworking shop into what was once used as a family room in a split level home. In order to make this 420 sq. ft. shop function, I've had to put most machines on wheels. Mobility allows me to configure the shop for a variety of tasks, from rough milling long boards to creating a space for spray finishing. It's not ideal, but with four windows and finished walls, it's a lot more pleasant than my former cinder-block basement shop.

Like the authors whose work is featured in this book, I've made every effort to get the most out of my shop. Layout, storage solutions, choice of tools, dust collection and safety were all important considerations in its evolution.

Aesthetics are important too. When I moved into my shop, I figured the obnoxious pink-toned walls would eventually be hidden by a fine layer of sawdust. Despite my best efforts, the pink held on like a bad case of red eye. After three years, I finally painted the walls and floor, too. As a bonus, the paint job helped me see better due to

the more reflective, neutral colors surrounding me.

My shop isn't really done; it's continually evolving, like that of most woodworkers, and I'm always looking for new ideas. The articles in this book are intended to offer solutions on everything from the big picture issues of design and workflow to the nitty gritty of picking the right tools. Orig-

inally published in *Fine Woodworking* magazine, these articles represent the innovative spirit of woodworkers everywhere, in shops large and small.

Anatole Burkin
Editor
Fine Woodworking

The Shop as Tool

BY JOE TRACY

A well-designed, well-built shop can do more for your woodworking than any new tablesaw or handplane. A good shop is a place you want to be—a safe, comfortable, well-lit space where work flows efficiently from machine to bench to finishing area. Of course, building a shop is a more expensive proposition than buying a new tablesaw. Whatever your situation—even if you just want to retrofit a basement or garage—you won't go wrong if you think of your shop as a complex functioning tool that calls for continual sharpening and adjustment.

The first step in creating a new workshop is determining a floor plan that will make it an efficient and enjoyable place to work. You don't want your tools simply lining the walls of the shop. Instead, consider not only the area that the tool will take up but also what I call a tool's shadow—the amount of space around the tool that will make it accessible for ripping and crosscutting. Because my two tablesaws see more work than any of my other machines, I wanted them in central locations, but within proximity to the lumber room. I also wanted them in relatively permanent locations, but in places where I could reposition them to accommodate large or awkward boards.

No matter how big a shop is, materials and projects will sooner or later have it straining at its seams. Flexible use of space is very important to me. Unless something is being used, I want it out of the way. The best solution to a problem is often just at the edge of our conceptual reach—disarmingly simple sometimes, but requiring a creative leap. The drawings and photos show just a few of the ways I've managed to capitalize on shop space.

Building Plans

When I set out to build my shop six years ago, I had a number of ideas I wanted to incorporate into the structure. I decided early on to use metal agricultural roofing, a relatively inexpensive roofing material that's durable and sheds snow well, which is not an insignificant consideration here in Maine.

I framed the roof to provide deep eaves to keep as much snow, rain, and sun away from the sides and base of the building as possible. Not only does this help protect siding, all but eliminating the need for maintenance, but it also provides storage space beneath the eaves, next to the walls of the shop.

Almost all of my windows are shopbuilt. When I made them, I sized them to

fit precisely between the wall studs for easy installation. I also placed the windows high up on the wall, near the eaves, so I have plenty of wall space inside for shelving and hanging tools—not to mention that the natural light they provide is a welcome boon to any shop.

Shop Layout

Once inside the shop, milling of stock takes place in one section of the shop, bench work elsewhere, and sanding and finishing in still other locations. Dust can be a nuisance, as well as a health hazard, and handling it is a chore. I placed all my sanding machines—a stroke sander, disk sander, inflatable drum sander and reciprocating spindle sander—in one corner, and use a simple exhaust fan to keep dust away from other machines. I also outfitted all my major machines—the shaper, jointer, planer, and my two tablesaws—with ducts for dust collection. The stroke sander has its own dust-collection system, and all the dust barrels are kept near doorways so they're easy to carry out and dump.

Once you get a rough idea of how you want your shop to look and function, the lay of the land begins to fill in some of the details. I sell my furniture from my shop, so the southeast corner—with its abundance of sunlight and attractive position as you approach the building—was the obvious choice for the showroom.

The location of the lumber room seemed just as logical. It's in the rear of the shop where it's easily accessible from the driveway. Boards move smoothly—on good days—from one end of the shop to the other. Overall, it's a great shop, but there's always room to improve. My next one will be even better.

JOE TRACY works wood on Mount Desert Island, Maine. With over 30 years of woodworking experience, he has built everything from production furniture to timber-frame houses.

Paying attention to details while keeping the big picture in mind helps you stay out of hot water.

The Intentional Shop

The author's second shop incorporates all he learned from his first effort. A scale model helped him work out proportions and details.

1. FINISHING ROOM

I hung an interior wall on four heavy-duty door hinges. The wall closes, making space for assembly, storage, or anything else. But when it's open, it forms an efficient little spray booth. An exhaust fan keeps finish odors away from other areas of the shop.

2. VACUUM PRESS

On one side of the finishing room's movable wall is my vacuum veneer press table, a hinged table on a hinged wall. When the table is needed, it drops down, but most of the time, it is folded against the wall, out of the way.

3. LUMBER STORAGE

The driveway runs up to the lumber storage area, which comes in handy when unloading wood.

4. GARAGE DOOR

Inside, I store long boards vertically, so I can get to them without unstacking a pile. I modified a garage door so it opens almost straight up—this leaves high wall space for storing boards.

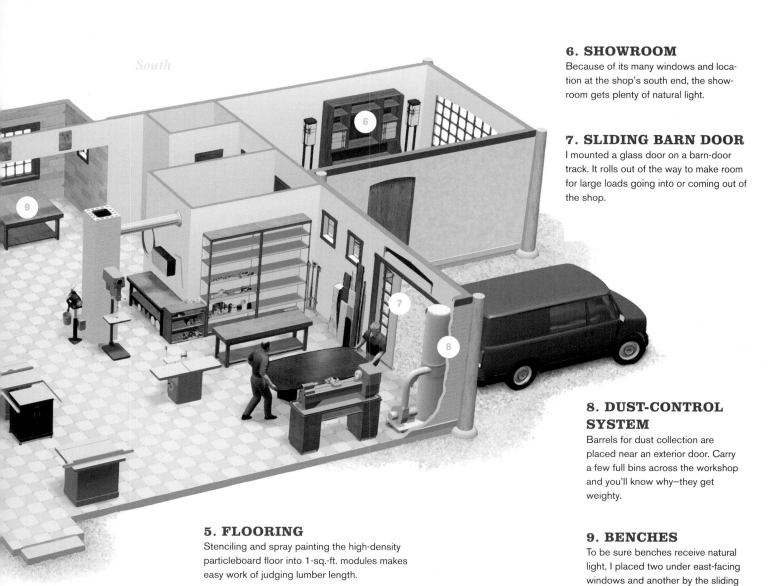

6. SHOWROOM

Because of its many windows and location at the shop's south end, the showroom gets plenty of natural light.

7. SLIDING BARN DOOR

I mounted a glass door on a barn-door track. It rolls out of the way to make room for large loads going into or coming out of the shop.

8. DUST-CONTROL SYSTEM

Barrels for dust collection are placed near an exterior door. Carry a few full bins across the workshop and you'll know why—they get weighty.

5. FLOORING

Stenciling and spray painting the high-density particleboard floor into 1-sq.-ft. modules makes easy work of judging lumber length.

9. BENCHES

To be sure benches receive natural light, I placed two under east-facing windows and another by the sliding glass door.

Components of a Smart Shop

Imagination and modification of surrounding materials make the author's shop both versatile and efficient.

DOOR STAYS OUT OF THE WAY. The author modified a regular garage door; otherwise, it would have made moving and sorting boards in the vertical storage area difficult. He hacksawed a kerf in the tracks the door rides in, then straightened and oriented them almost vertically. Counterweighting the door makes it easy to open.

A DISAPPEARING ROUTER TABLE. Built for convenience, the author's router table can be clamped in a bench vise and ready to use in seconds. It stores out of the way just as quickly.

SAVING A TOOL. The author's bandsaw was bought from an old warehouse for $40 and then reworked. The author made a plywood case for the bottom and used old sash weights to counterweight the guidepost, making it easier to adjust.

MISTER KEEPS TOOLS COOL. Powered by compressed air, this mister blasts coolant from the reservoir onto the grinder pedestal and leading edge of the tool being ground, preventing the tool from being burned.

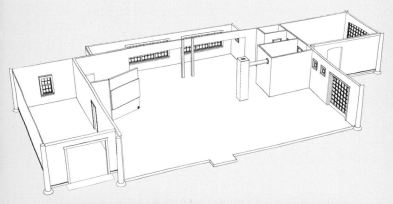

SMALL TOUCHES ADD COMFORT TO A SHOP. With the author's vacuum press folded away in the movable wall, you see that a quick paint job on a simple particleboard floor breaks up the monotony of the shop. Beneath the particleboard are 2x4 sleepers and radiant-heat tubing that comes out at his feet, where it does the most good.

A DOOR TO EASE THE LOAD. A large door on a barn-door track slides open to make awkward loads more manageable. The author opted for a glass door to keep the shop well-lit.

Great Shop in a Two-Car Garage

BY CURTIS ERPELDING

A workshop ought to be practical—a place to work wood and to keep tools and materials dry and warm—but it never is. That's because it is also very personal. The problems you solve as you outfit your shop may be practical ones, but they arise for personal reasons: You make jigsaw puzzles as well as highboys; your shop is unheated in the winter and floods in the spring; you like to stand while drawing and sit down while cutting dovetails; you store your kayak for half the year suspended from the ceiling above your milling machines.

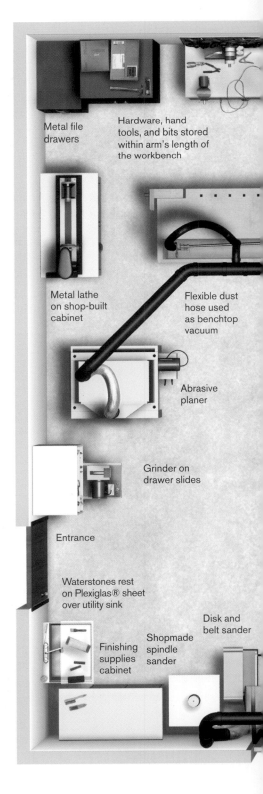

Metal file drawers

Hardware, hand tools, and bits stored within arm's length of the workbench

Metal lathe on shop-built cabinet

Flexible dust hose used as benchtop vacuum

Abrasive planer

Grinder on drawer slides

Entrance

Waterstones rest on Plexiglas® sheet over utility sink

Disk and belt sander

Finishing supplies cabinet

Shopmade spindle sander

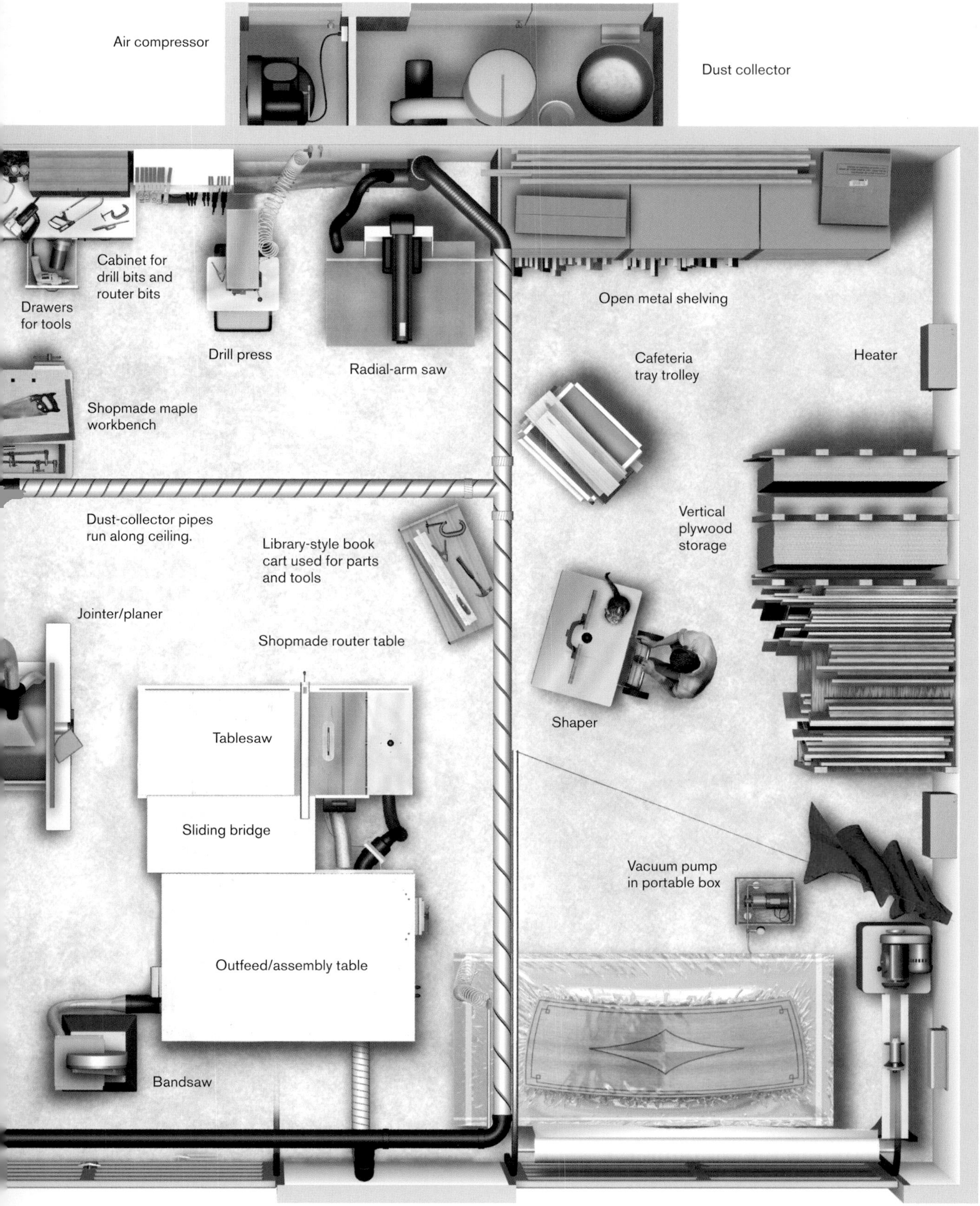

Air compressor

Dust collector

Cabinet for
drill bits and
router bits

Drawers
for tools

Drill press

Radial-arm saw

Shopmade maple
workbench

Open metal shelving

Cafeteria
tray trolley

Heater

Dust-collector pipes
run along ceiling.

Library-style book
cart used for parts
and tools

Vertical
plywood
storage

Jointer/planer

Shopmade router table

Tablesaw

Shaper

Sliding bridge

Outfeed/assembly table

Vacuum pump
in portable box

Bandsaw

One corner of
the shop has
five uses:

Vacuum
veneering
(table knocks
down)

Spraying finish
(tarp creates
booth with
exhaust fan)

Turning (lathe
covered when
not in use)

Photography
(backdrop
hangs from
door tracks)

Plywood deliv-
ery (the truck
backs right in)

The Heart of the Shop

With all the room a tablesaw requires for infeed, outfeed, and support on either side of the blade, its placement is the logical starting point for laying out a shop. The author decided to make his outfeed table do double duty as a fixed-in-place assembly table. A sliding bridge connects the saw with the assembly table.

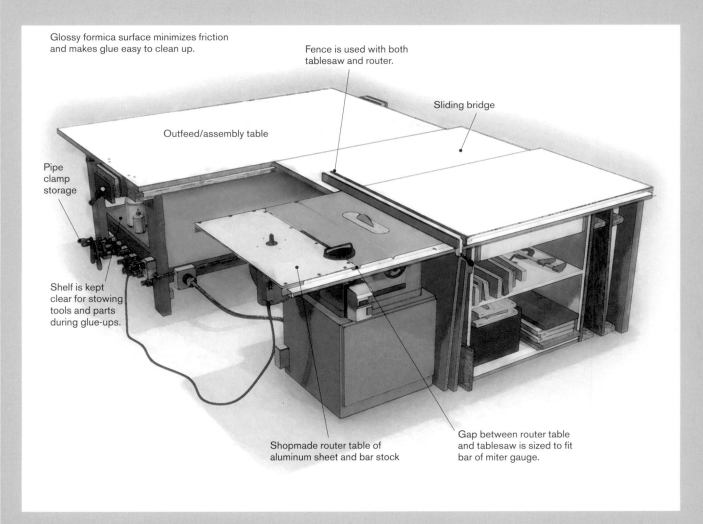

Glossy formica surface minimizes friction and makes glue easy to clean up.

Fence is used with both tablesaw and router.

Sliding bridge

Outfeed/assembly table

Pipe clamp storage

Shelf is kept clear for stowing tools and parts during glue-ups.

Shopmade router table of aluminum sheet and bar stock

Gap between router table and tablesaw is sized to fit bar of miter gauge.

Bridge is the key to the system

With bridge pushed to the right you can:

- use crosscut sled.
- use clamps to fix jigs on tablesaw or router table.
- gain access to tablesaw motor and dust-collector port.

- have three-sided support for cutting sheet goods with a circular saw, sabersaw, or router.

Bridge is slid to the left for ripping. Bridge lifts out completely for walking access behind assembly table.

In a Small Shop, Most Things Should Be Movable

When machines and tools can be moved for different situations, it allows for a more comfortable work environment. While some tools are used less often than others, it helps to have the option of creating more space when it's needed.

TILT AND ROLL

LIFT AND ROLL

LET IT SLIDE

STATIONARY DISK AND BELT SANDER has wheels just off the floor, so you can tip it back and move it like a wheelbarrow. Offset, nonswivel casters are key.

A PAIR OF NONSWIVEL, HEAVY-DUTY CASTERS make the shaper movable, and a pair of adjustable glides keep it level and stable. For a long move, a hand truck helps. The cat provides good ballast.

THE JOINTER/PLANER often needs to be angled to increase feed clearance. A simple plywood box with nail-in glides at the corners makes a stable, slidable base.

I've had six shops over the last 20 years, and I've found that improving a shop is a matter of learning about myself and the way I work, both in general and in each specific space.

In my first shop, which was the cleared-out end of a book-storage warehouse, I hung the few tools I had accumulated on the wall a good 10 paces away from my worktable. It soon became apparent that constant trips between the wall and the worktable were doing nothing for my productivity. I learned a specific lesson and applied it in my succeeding shops: Store drill bits by the drill press, sawblades by the saw, hand tools by the workbench, jigs and fixtures by the machines they were built for.

I also learned a more general rule of shop design: You'll rarely get it right the first time. It takes time and experience to create a well-functioning, efficient shop. All of the aspects of shop order—from tool and machine layout to work-flow procedures and storage solutions—evolve over time.

My grinding setup is an example of Darwinism as it applies in the workshop. In that first shop, my grinding device was a hand-operated wheel clamped to the edge of the table. It had all the disadvantages: It was slow, it took muscle, its minimal tool rest made it difficult to obtain a consistent edge and, being clamped to the worktable, it was in the way. It didn't take too long to realize that if I was serious about making a living while using hand tools, I would have to find a better system.

The first improvement was to motorize. I salvaged an old washing-machine motor that ran at a convenient 1,725 rpm and fitted it with a white vitrified wheel. Then I went about finding a better approach to the tool-rest problem. One drawback of most tool rests is that they don't fully support the blade being sharpened. Another problem is that they force you to hold the tool or blade at

an unnatural angle. I built a tool rest in the shape of an open-sided box around the grinding wheel. The wheel emerges through a slot in the top of the box the way a table-saw blade emerges through the throat plate. This enables me to grind tools while they are lying flat and fully supported on the top of the box (see left photo on p. 16). Even spokeshave irons and small marking knives can be precisely ground without the need for positioning fixtures. With the motor mounted on a hinged board, I can adjust the grinding angle by raising or lowering the motor. That was my second sharpening setup, permanently mounted at the end of a wall bench. My current arrangement has the same grinder, but the box is now mounted on the wall at a comfortable height for grinding. The whole mechanism is on drawer slides and is pulled out of the box for use. This saves space but also keeps dust, debris, and stray tools from ending up on the grinder.

Because everything evolves, being flexible is another inflexible rule of organization. Try not to make any feature of the shop permanent. The arrival of new tools, new types of work, or simply better ideas will demand a new arrangement.

Having machines that are movable is particularly advantageous in a small shop. In my own shop spaces, I've kept my machinery small. One of the advantages of having small, lightweight machines is that you can easily move them, even by yourself. With my 14-in. bandsaw, for example, I don't have room for the optimal 8 ft. or 10 ft. of clearance on the outfeed side. In good weather, I increase outfeed clearance by opening the garage door. In poor weather, I simply pivot the machine. With heavier machines, I improvise. I mounted two non-swivel casters and two adjustable glides inside the base of my shaper. They raise the machine $\frac{1}{8}$ in. or so, without compromising its stability. I can

Nearby Drawers Improve the Bench

The author worked for years with his bench against a wall. Moving the bench away from the wall and building a cabinet with drawers behind it made him far more productive.

1. Pulled away from the wall, the bench can be used from both sides, and workpieces can extend from it in all directions.

2. With counter space and tool storage within arm's length, the workbench stays uncluttered.

3. Cabinet is used for router bits and drill bits.

4. Countertop with laminate surface and integral splash is available in various lengths at home centers. This 8-ft. section cost about $50.

5. Deep drawers run on heavy-duty, full-extension slides and hold routers, drills, sanders, and air tools.

Savvy Retrofit
and Reuse

From the Lunchroom to the Workshop

For $50, the author bought an aluminum trolley for cafeteria trays. A good scrubbing and some ½-in. flakeboard shelves turned it into a parts cart.

Pump House

A quick plywood box, with cutout handles and a slide-in lid, makes a snug mobile home for the author's vacuum-veneering pump. When not in use, it is stored on a shelf.

Revive-a-Vac

The bottom half of a dead shop vacuum makes a rolling rag bin, trash can, or a barrel for cutoffs. A scrap of flakeboard placed on top turns it into a utility table for mixing finishes.

Gliding Grinder

This grinder slides out of a box for use. For rigidity, two pairs of drawer slides are used: one pair side-mounting, the other bottom-mounting. The open box around the grinding wheel is the tool rest, which enables the author to grind blades while holding them flat. The blades ride on a steel wear plate. The motor mount is hinged, and changing its height adjusts the grinding angle.

move it short distances by lifting the side with the glides and pushing or pulling. For longer trips, I use a hand truck to lift and push the side with the glides. I could have bought a mobile base for the shaper, but I didn't want to raise the shaper significantly because I use it as a side support when I crosscut long pieces on the tablesaw.

Because each shop presents unique problems, it makes sense to make your own shop fittings and furniture. But that doesn't mean you can't find ready-made solutions. I have an old, large metal cabinet full of drawers. It was originally used for storing Addressograph printing plates, and it was free for the hauling. I spent a couple of hours modifying the drawer interiors, and it is now brimming with neatly segregated screws, sandpaper, hardware, and glue. All sorts of card file cabinets are obsolete as a result of the computer revolution. The cabinets range from the fine wooden ones with dovetailed drawers that libraries used for their card catalogs to standing metal cabinets and two- or four-drawer desktop cases.

Used office-furniture stores are a good place to haunt. Metal file-drawer cabinets in legal or letter size make fine storage for mid-size items, and used ones can be had quite cheaply. And at a bankruptcy sale, I bought a metal storage rack for $20 that would have cost me at least a day of labor and $100 in materials to duplicate in wood.

Being a frugal sort, I like the idea of adaptive reuse. Two of my roll-around carts are sturdy aluminum trolleys that used to carry cafeteria trays. I bought them for $50

apiece at a scrap-metal yard. I scrubbed them down and cut pieces of $\frac{1}{2}$-in. particleboard to use as shelves where the trays once went. These 6-ft.-high carts, with their footprint of $1\frac{1}{2}$-ft. by $2\frac{1}{2}$-ft., can hold an enormous number of furniture parts that would otherwise be scattered over tables or benchtops or spilling onto the floor.

Like all shops, mine is a stage for the eternal battle between order and chaos. And true to thermodynamic law, chaos has the edge. As years go by, I collect more jigs and fixtures that somehow can't be thrown out, extra material from each job begins to add up, and, of course, I can't resist that extra piece of equipment. The more I try to squeeze in, the more chaos threatens to take over. At some point, after all the space-saving devices have been deployed, the issue becomes paring back (perish the thought) or expanding the space. This spring, after working in a two-car garage for six years, I am remodeling the shop, nearly doubling the working area. I have a pretty good idea how I'll use this added space—a dedicated finishing room, a fold-up table for vacuum veneering, a place where the lathe is more accessible. Whether these ideas will work out as planned I don't know. But I am certain that over time my needs will change, my accessories will increase, the new space will evolve to accommodate them, and chaos will slowly regain its lost ground.

CURTIS ERPELDING is a furniture maker living in Port Orchard, Wash.

The Almost Perfect Basement Shop

BY JAN CARR

A basement is hardly the most desirable location for a shop. Yet, for many woodworkers, it's the only alternative. I live in a city, and even if expense were not an issue, there is simply no space for a separate outbuilding. Furthermore, living in a cold climate, a shop in the garage is problematic to say the least.

When my wife and I moved to Minnesota some years ago, we looked for a house that was a candidate for renovation. From my point of view, I wanted a house with a good potential for setting up a shop.

So when we found this house in St. Paul with a large basement sporting 8-ft. ceilings and a separate outside entrance, the rest of the structure looked pretty good to me. With all the renovation work looming, I chose to build the shop first. What follows is an account of what I did and why, with the hope that this discussion will help others develop a strategy that works for them.

Making the Space Habitable

I am a researcher by inclination. When confronted with a problem for which I know of no clear-cut answers—for example, the best way to insulate basement walls—I try to confer with at least five people or sources for the answer. I look for a consensus, if there is any, but mostly use common sense to weigh the options toward a decision. Pablo Picasso supposedly said that all art is derivative; that is, a by-product of others' ideas. That is certainly true in the case of my shop. Nearly every concept of shop design that I've incorporated into my space came through a process by which I saw someone else's idea, then revised, adapted, or tweaked it to meet my own needs.

Before moving to St. Paul, we lived in a loft in New York City, where I appropriated a finished bedroom for shop space. Though it was small, that shop was extraordinarily

ONCE YOU GET PAST THE DOG, getting into this shop is easy. A separate entrance (at left) into the basement from the street level facilitates bringing lumber and plywood into this organized and comfortable workspace.

comfortable. Once in Minnesota, we spent our first year in a rented house, where I set up shop in a dark, dank, thoroughly depressing basement. Those two experiences convinced me to do whatever was necessary to make this new shop as pleasant as possible. That meant erecting insulated stud walls, installing ceilings, and painting floors and walls. Birch plywood was available for about $30 per sheet at the time, so I hung my tools on stained and varnished birch panels and built simple birch cabinets that were tailored to my storage needs.

Dealing with Moisture and Ventilation

Any basement with stone or concrete walls will be cold in the winter and damp in the summer, at least in the northern tier of North America. Most states and many localities have some sort of energy-information center that will help you solve the problems common to your area. The energy people in Minnesota gave me detailed guidelines for erecting insulated stud walls with a continuous vapor barrier, which I did on all of the exterior walls. That alone made a substantial

dent in our heating bills and rendered the space comfortable through the notoriously cold winters.

In the summer I put screens on the windows and use some cheap 8-in. box fans to provide cross ventilation. Also, I run two 40-pint dehumidifiers during the summer. These devices are expensive to operate—each about equal to what a refrigerator costs to run—but they keep the shop dry and comfortable. I have never had any problems with rusted tools or warped boards, so the dehumidifiers seem well worth the expense to me.

Lights: Incandescent vs. Fluorescent

Take an informal poll, and you'll find that hardly anyone prefers the look of fluorescent light to incandescent, but you simply can't beat it on cost and output. I wanted a shop with bright, shadowless illumination, a factor of increasing importance to those of us with the diminishing eyesight that comes with advancing years.

I haven't had good luck with the so-called shop lights available from most home centers for about $8, because they're too noisy. So I bought standard 4-ft. two-bulb fixtures at about twice that price. You can eliminate the ubiquitous hum of the fixtures by going with electronic ballasts (at about $37 per fixture). However, an electrician friend of mine suggested that I return any of the standard fixtures that hummed, because the quality control over ballasts is pretty abysmal. I found about one in three to be defective. As a result, my shop lights are reasonably quiet.

Bulb selection is also important. A lighting expert I talked with suggested the best bulbs for accurate color rendition should be rated at about 3,500° on the Kelvin scale. That's what I installed in the shop, even though each bulb cost about $2.50 at a local electrical-supply house. The result is a pleasant light that to me is infinitely preferable to those cool-white bulbs you can pick up for a buck apiece.

Keep the Noise Down Unless you want to outfit other members of your family with ear protection, you probably need to think about shop noise. There are any number of measures you can employ to inhibit sound transmission, but most are rather elaborate and expensive.

I decided to take the simplest route, which was to stuff conventional fiberglass insulation between the rafters and use resilient channels (sometimes available from home centers but always from drywall suppliers) to attach the ceiling drywall. This will not stop all of the sound from drifting upward, but it does bring the roar of machines and tools down to a more tolerable level.

Organizing for Efficiency

After you've finished whatever decorating you've chosen to do, the sometimes daunting process of organizing your space begins in earnest. Most experts will tell you to think about workflow in setting up your space. That's difficult advice to follow in a basement, given the fixed obstructions, such as chimneys, support columns, and heating and plumbing fixtures. As a consequence, you are often forced to organize around these various obstructions and give secondary consideration to the logical flow of work. I knew that most of my shop time would be devoted to renovation tasks such as stripping doors and moldings and building case goods. With that in mind, I located the tablesaw first so that there would be adequate space to cut sheet goods and maintain an open area for stripping.

It makes sense to draw a simple floor plan of the available space. I've found it useful to make scale drawings of the machines, as well as some of the materials you expect to work, such as 4x8 sheets of plywood. You can then move your machines around on the floor plan to determine which placement gives you the most space to work the materials.

Layout, Cockpit Style From my days in an office, I came to favor what I think of as a cockpit work environment—sitting at a desk with my necessary office machines and work materials in a U shape around my back and sides. I took that same idea to the shop. As I work at the tablesaw, my workbench is to my left, the tool wall is to my right, and necessary hardware and portable power tools are right behind me (see the floor plan at right). For 90% of my work in the shop, everything I need is within two steps. I left enough room in the middle of this space to assemble cabinets.

Keep the Space Flexible Given the obstructions and space limitations of most basements, consider making as many items movable as you can. In my shop, everything can be broken down or moved, with the exception of the benches and the tablesaw. The challenge with machines, of course, is to make them movable, and then—when in use—immobile. I've tried a variety of devices over the years, but my current favorite is the

Making the Space Work

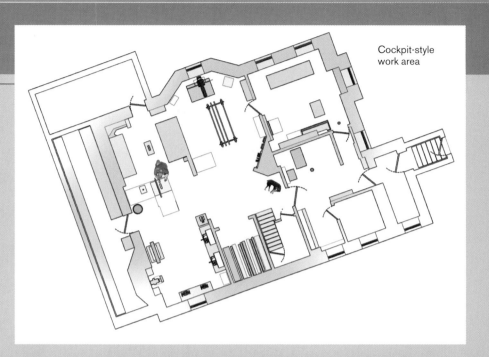

Cockpit-style work area

Blessed with a large basement to begin with, the
author improved its efficiency by
ganging together specific areas
for tool storage and workflow.

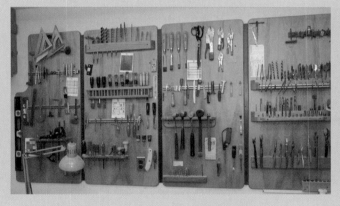

**1. EVERY TOOL HAS ITS PLACE. The author chose birch plywood
over Peg-Board® to make wall panels and storage cabinets for
all of his tools.**

**2. CLEARLY A SHARED SPACE. Laundry-room walls double as
storage space for brushes and detergent.**

**3. THERE ARE FEW SHADOWS ON THIS
WORKBENCH. A stickler for plentiful light,
the author ran 4-ft. fixtures continuously
along the ceiling in closely spaced rows.
All told, he spent about $650 for 26 fix-
tures and color-correct bulbs.**

**4. SMALL FANS THROW PLENTY OF AIR.
This window fan, mounted above the
sharpening station, exhausts air blown in
by a fan on the opposite wall. The two
small fans keep the air from getting stale.**

**5. DEHUMIDIFIERS HELP PREVENT RUST
ON TOOLS. Two of these devices run continuously from June through August to
keep the space dry during humid
weather. This one doubles as a support
for a chopsaw workstation.**

A Knockdown Utility Table That Sets Up in No Time

Two sawhorses and three lengths of 2x4s provide me with a quick, no-fuss worktable when I need one. I use it for cutting panels, assembling casework, and drying finished work. Half-lap joints make this table easy to put together and take apart. It stores readily out of the way.

2x4 to hold it all together. I use this as a cutting rack for plywood, as an assembly bench, and, with a sheet of plywood on the top, as a general utility table. And if I need the floor space, the whole thing can be pulled apart and moved aside in about 10 seconds.

Match Bench Heights to Fit You also need to think about the height of your machines. The top surface of my tablesaw is 34 in. off the floor, which, in turn, determined the height of nearby benches, so I can slide a sheet of plywood over the bench onto the tablesaw. Conversely, the jointer/planer sits at a lower height so that pieces of lumber will slip under the saw's extension table.

A Work in Progress

In many respects, designing and building a shop will be the most complicated project most woodworkers will ever undertake. As such, it can be intimidating if you are as compulsive as I am and want to get it right the first time. However, somewhere along the line, it dawned on me that a shop should be treated more as a work in progress than as a project to be completed. Thus liberated, I felt more comfortable in trying some new arrangement or idea and discarding it if it didn't work as well as I had originally hoped. Any number of my friends seem to find use for my rejects, and there have been many.

All of which is to suggest that you don't spend too much time or effort trying to devise the ideal shop. Start somewhere and just accept the inevitable reality that you will reconfigure again . . . and again . . . and again. Even now, on my drawing board, I'm trying to come up with another arrangement that would accommodate a dust collector, a 20-in. bandsaw, and a shaper.

JAN CARR builds cabinets and restores the three-story, turn-of-the-century home he shares with his wife in St. Paul, Minn.

universal mobile machine base made by Delta® (available for about $50).

One of the most adaptable devices in the shop is what I call the cutting rack (see sidebar above). It's simply a knock-down table, consisting of two sawhorses and three 2x4s, with half-lap joints between the top of each horse and each

Turning a Parking Place into a Great Shop Space

BY CHRIS GOCHNOUR

When my wife and I bought our house 15 years ago, I set up my first real shop in the freestanding two-car garage. Built in the 1940s, the garage was 18 ft. by 20 ft., with a concrete slab and wood siding. I entered and exited through the overhead garage doors, attempted to heat the space with electric radiators, and worked with low ceilings, no insulation, a lot of airborne dust and very little natural light. I loved it. At least for a while. As I acquired more tools and machines, the space quickly became crowded. In the mean time, I had quit my job and begun making furniture full time. When I took that step, I realized I needed to retrofit the shop completely. I took the opportunity not just to enlarge the space but to revamp the layout using all that I'd learned about the way I work.

Several core decisions have made my shop a pleasant and efficient place to work. Most important, I divided the shop's layout according to the three main activities of my

A Well-Designed Shop

The author expanded a typical two-car garage shop, doubling the space by adding on at the back. As he rebuilt and rearranged the shop, he based his decisions on aesthetics as well as efficiency, creating a space that is a pleasure to work in.

Finish room

Scissors trusses create vaulted ceiling.

Plywood floor takes spills without complaint.

Bench area

Solid-oak plank floor is easy on feet and dropped tools.

Sanding station

Assembly table with drawers

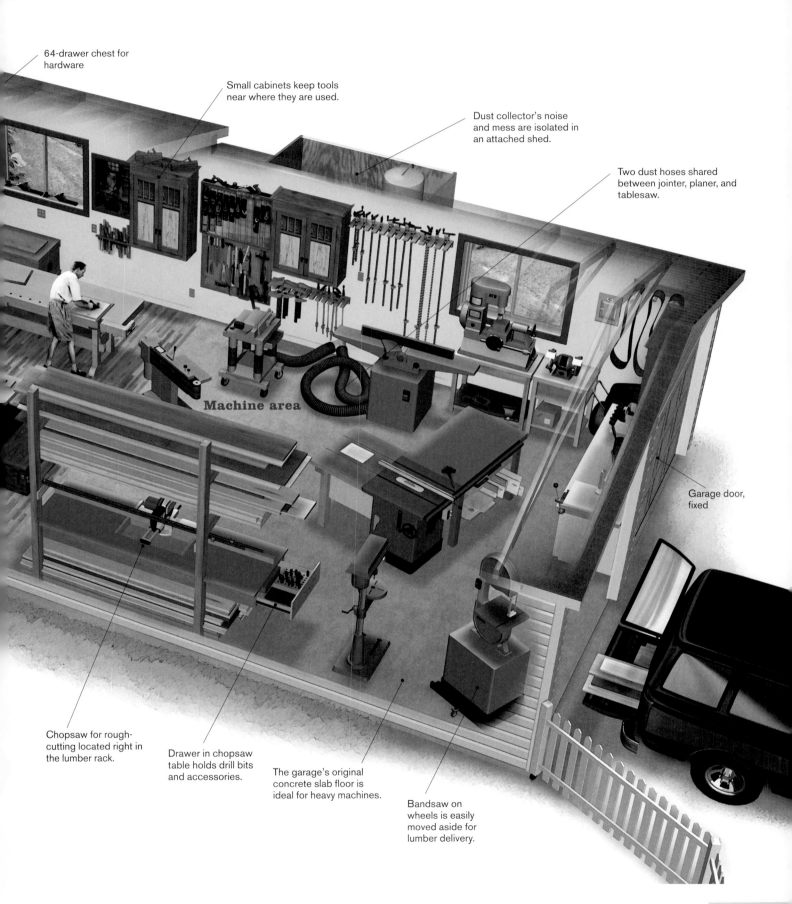

64-drawer chest for hardware

Small cabinets keep tools near where they are used.

Dust collector's noise and mess are isolated in an attached shed.

Two dust hoses shared between jointer, planer, and tablesaw.

Machine area

Garage door, fixed

Chopsaw for rough-cutting located right in the lumber rack.

Drawer in chopsaw table holds drill bits and accessories.

The garage's original concrete slab floor is ideal for heavy machines.

Bandsaw on wheels is easily moved aside for lumber delivery.

THE TABLESAW IS KING. **In the
machine area, the tablesaw
stands fixed near the center,
and the other machines are
arranged around it.**

work: machine work, bench work, and finishing. Then, within those three areas, I
arranged the machines and tools to reflect
the flow of work while keeping the layout
as fluid as possible so that it could be
changed to accommodate different projects.
To store hand tools, hardware, and accessories for various machines, I built a number of smaller cabinets rather than several
large ones. This enabled me to place tools
and equipment right where they are most
often used. I also put a lot of effort into
aesthetic improvements. For instance, I took
the time to build handsome cabinets for
tool storage instead of whacking them
together from scrap.

Most of the ideas I've built my shop
around can be adapted to any workspace.
Even so, I don't expect them all to suit
yours, because designing a personal workshop is just that—personal. The best design
is the one that responds directly to the way
you work. But I've put a lot of effort into
the slow process of evolving my shop, and I
hope you'll find some tips here that help.

Enlarging My Garage

Because the lot is small and my budget was
modest, it made sense to enlarge the garage
rather than to put up a separate shop building. I started the renovation by making my
best decision first: I chose not to tackle the
whole job myself. As a furniture maker, I

may be familiar with a carpenter's tools, but that doesn't make me a carpenter. So I hired a contractor friend and signed myself up as a laborer.

The roof was the key to the renovation. We replaced the old rafters and collar ties with scissors trusses, and where I used to have a flat 8-ft. ceiling, I suddenly had a ceiling that is 8 ft. at the side walls and rises to 11 ft. at the center. Hallelujah.

Along with a higher ceiling, the renovated shop has far better lighting. The first improvement came with installing two large windows in the bench area. The added natural light throughout the shop helps with color matching and simply makes me feel better. In addition, instead of reinstalling the suspended fluorescent lights I had before, I recessed some fluorescent fixtures in the ceiling and covered them with Lexan®. This was a miraculous improvement—it looked much better, provided even illumination, and meant there'd be no more whacking of dust-laden light fixtures with the end of a board.

To help retain the heat (and the noise), I added better wall insulation and replaced the old garage doors with insulated metal ones. I installed a basic dust-collection system, placing the collector outside in a small shed attached to the building, which reduces the noise and makes it less messy to empty. I supplemented the dust collector with a ceiling-mounted dust filter.

In the end, the only parts of the original shop that were preserved were the concrete slab floor and the front and side walls. The whole job took about seven weeks and cost about $13,000. Although I can't claim that the outlay was painless, in most ways the renovation was extremely low-impact. Even though the headroom had increased dramatically and the floor space had doubled to 720 sq. ft., if you were looking at the garage from the street, you'd never guess that anything had changed.

Machine Area

The space once occupied by automobiles became my machine area. It was in the right place in terms of workflow—just inside the overhead doors—and it had a good floor for heavy machines: the garage's original concrete slab.

All of my work starts with rough lumber, so I built my lumber rack near the one still-operable garage door, along the side wall. When I buy lumber, I back my truck up to the garage door and unload the wood directly onto the rack. The rack I made has a pair of vertical posts bolted to the wall and support arms cantilevered from the posts. This provides unobstructed access to the wood and takes up the least possible space in the shop.

I use a chopsaw for rough-cutting lumber to length, and I wanted it right where the lumber was. So I cleared out a shelf of lumber and used the same cantilevered support system to hang a chopsaw table. I built the table using torsion-box construction and attached the chopsaw to a small, removable section at the middle of the table. When I need the saw on an installation, I simply unscrew two bolts and lift the saw and its small platform out of the table.

In arranging the major machines, I started by placing the tablesaw, with its huge demands for infeed, outfeed, and side support, in the center of the machine space. All of the other machines were placed on the periphery, arranged to work in harmony with the tablesaw.

Whenever feasible, I put my machines on wheels. Flexibility in the layout of a small shop is imperative, and wheels help tremendously with this. I have all of my major standing machines on wheels except for my tablesaw and jointer.

The jointer and planer are near the tablesaw, which makes sense from the perspective of workflow, and it also helps with dust collection. Arranged this way,

other is a broad assembly table. Having the two in proximity—they are parallel and stand about 6 ft. apart—is extremely functional. Both are movable (with some effort), and I can change their locations depending on what I am building.

Whereas the cabinetmaker's bench is open underneath, the assembly table is packed solid: I utilized the large space beneath the top by filling it with cabinets and heavy-duty drawers. These hold all of my handheld power tools and their accessories and much hardware. This way, the tools are stored within arm's length of where they are used. The drawers are also easily reached from the workbench. The assembly table has several outlets built in under the top, and I added one to the workbench as well.

these three primary generators of dust can share the two hoses that I have hooked up to my dust collector. In my old shop, I had ceiling-mounted PVC pipe running to every machine. I found it to be overkill, and it produced enough static electricity to keep my hair standing on end much of the time. These days I simply have flexible hose running on the floor. It may be a slight nuisance to step over, but it works fine, is a more adaptable system, and doesn't mess with my hair.

The tablesaw took precedence not only in laying out the machine area but also in my tool budget. My theory of machine purchases is this: For machines I use most heavily and rely on most for precision work—tablesaw, jointer, planer, mortiser, pin-router—I cough up the money for high-quality, heavy-duty equipment. For more peripheral machines, where accuracy is less critical—edge sander, grinder, dust collector—I tend toward Taiwanese knockoffs.

Bench Area

The two main work surfaces in my bench area summarize the work I do there. One is a traditional cabinetmaker's bench, and the

Variations to Suit the Owner The cabinetmaker's bench is fairly traditional, but I did make a few departures. One was to leave out a tool trough in favor of a larger work surface. I built in a tail vise, which is invaluable, but in place of a traditional shoulder vise I opted for a commercial metal side vise. I find a shoulder vise to be a bit of an impediment, and these metal vises are hard to beat with their convenient quick release, great holding power, and easy installation.

Building my own bench meant I could design it for just the way I work. Working with handplanes a lot, as I do, a good, solid bench is almost as important as a sharp blade. You want all of your energy transferred into the workpiece and the cutting action—not into a rickety bench that racks and wobbles with every stroke.

For tools used primarily at the workbench, I built shallow, two-door cabinets and hung them on the wall by the bench. They store chisels, handplanes, scrapers, spokeshaves, and other supplies. Storing tools and supplies behind doors helps with dust problems, and keeping the cabinets shallow makes for simpler tool storage and retrieval.

Quality Throughout the Shop My approach to building storage cabinets is a little different from some. Instead of building shop furniture quickly and cheaply, I put real effort into building it. If I can save some labor or money, I do—two of the tool cabinets were extras from custom kitchens I built. But considering how much time I spend in my shop, it makes sense to please myself with the environment there. And the effort is not lost on clients who visit my shop. The cabinets demonstrate the type of work I do and the pride I take in my work and my tools.

My bench area has a third table, where I do most of my sanding. I may be a handplane fanatic, but I am practical enough to know that sanding is a reality. When I must sand, I want it to be as painless as possible. Thus, I built a dedicated sanding station. It is essentially a big box with a perforated top surface and a couple of vacuum motors below: One vacuum motor pulls the sanding dust down through a series of furnace filters; the other works as a hold-down system to keep the workpiece in place without clamps. The thing works so well that I don't need a dust mask, even when sanding with aggressive paper. I placed the station next to a window so that my time spent sanding is enriched by the changes of the seasons in my backyard. I still don't love sanding, but this device has certainly taken the sting out of it.

I put a hardwood floor in the bench area. The wood floor is easier on my feet and back than the concrete and more forgiving if I drop a tool. Better yet, the wood is honestly more inspiring to work on. I've even draped off a wall and used the bench area as a place to photograph my work.

Finish Room

I decided to separate the finish area from the rest of the shop, and I'm glad I did. Having it walled off keeps the dust in the workshop and the fumes in the finish room. I kept the ceilings high and installed large double doors that lead to the bench area. Even though the floor space in the finish room is fairly limited, the high ceilings and wide doorway make it easy to move even dining tables and tall case pieces in and out. It is also nice to be able to close the doors and not see the oversprayed walls and the clutter in there.

Perhaps as important as anything else in a finish room is the lighting. Two large windows let in natural light. The natural light helps in matching color when mixing stains and in seeing just how a coat of lacquer is laying down. And the windows, in combination with the door and an explosion-proof fan, provide good ventilation. I also have fluorescent lights recessed in the ceiling. To make them explosion-proof, I put the lights behind sheets of Lexan that are sealed at the perimeter with a rubber gasket. I also ran the switch to the bench area. To provide raking light for bringing out the details of a finish, I use a couple of portable halogen spotlights.

The floor in my finish room is just plywood. That way I don't feel so bad about lacquer overspray or stray splashes of pigments and stains. I keep all of my supplies in a metal cabinet and have a small work area for pouring and mixing finishes.

It has been six years now since I renovated the shop. With the added space, functional layout, and aesthetically pleasing surroundings, it's been a great place to make furniture. But the evolution continues. Future improvements include more windows, upgraded electrical service, and, perhaps most important, a better place for my wife to park her car.

CHRIS GOCHNOUR makes custom furniture and cabinets in Salt Lake City, Utah.

LUMBER AND A PLACE TO CUT IT. A system of cantilevered arms provides easy-access lumber storage as well as support for a chopsaw table designed for rough-cutting planks.

A Well-Organized One-Man Shop

BY ROSS DAY

The machine room of the shop has double sliding barn doors near the wood-storage areas. Weather stripping helps keep out drafts.

A light gray epoxy floor paint reflects light. Crushed walnut-shells were mixed with the paint to make a slip-free surface.

LAY OUT THE SHOP on graph paper. Draw machine and workbench footprints on separate pieces of paper and move them around to try different configurations.

Last year, my wife and I decided to leave the city for the country. Our goal was to buy a house, a shop building, and land so that we would no longer be at the mercy of downtown Seattle landlords and a real-estate market that had gone totally nuts. We found what we needed about an hour outside Seattle.

The shop building was a bare shell: concrete pad, open stud walls, no windows, and a lightbulb or two. It was large enough at 1,300 sq. ft. with a 12-ft. height from floor to trusses.

Having worked in a number of shops, I had a good idea of what I wanted: a design that maximized available space and efficiency in every way possible. To do that, I needed to think about workflow and storage and remember that floor space is precious. I aimed to keep the shop as uncluttered as possible, and that affected my choice of machinery. I also designed the shop with plenty of light, both natural and electric.

Draw It First, Then Pick Up the Hammer

I made a scale layout of the shop using ¼-in. graph-paper sheets taped together to represent my shop's 36-ft. by 36-ft. footprint (¼ in. = 1 ft.). Then I made scale footprints of all machines and benches—and whatever else would take up floor space—on separate pieces of paper.

Moving around these paper footprints let me try different combinations, locations, and workflow patterns, allowing me to visualize several workflow and storage combinations.

I prefer a shop that is divided into separate areas for machine work and for benchwork (see drawing on p. 32). However, I didn't want to lose the sense of spaciousness that this new building offered. My solution was twofold. The bench room received a raised wooden floor and was partially separated from the machine area by a floor-to-ceiling partition wall.

Machine and Bench Rooms Use Space Efficiently

The shop is divided approximately in half between the bench and machine rooms. I chose my machines for their efficiency and space-saving attributes. For example, I have a 12-in. short-stroke sliding tablesaw, which allows me to rip and crosscut on one machine. My

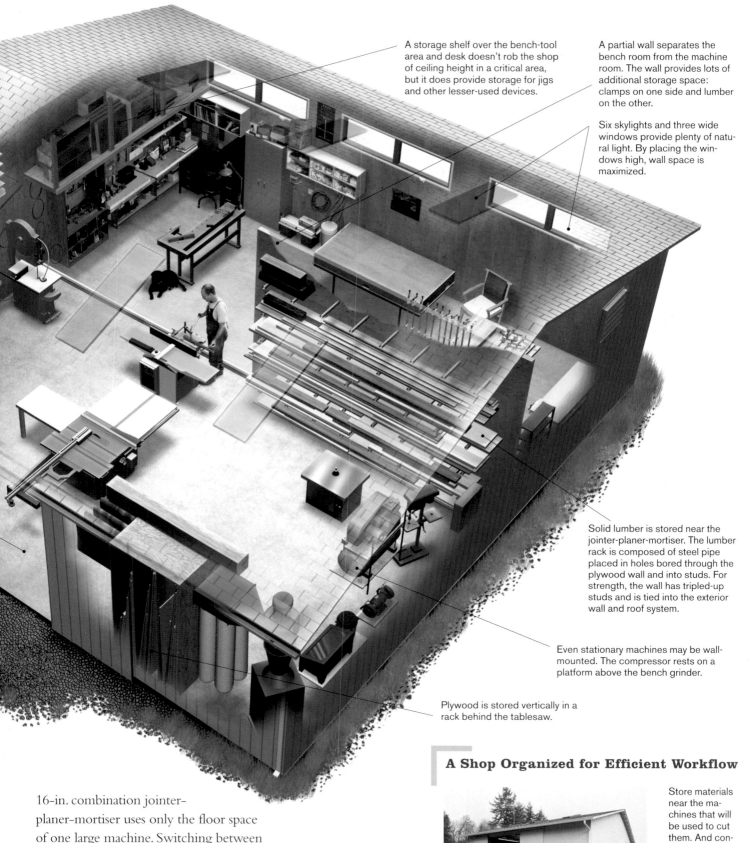

A storage shelf over the bench-tool area and desk doesn't rob the shop of ceiling height in a critical area, but it does provide storage for jigs and other lesser-used devices.

A partial wall separates the bench room from the machine room. The wall provides lots of additional storage space: clamps on one side and lumber on the other.

Six skylights and three wide windows provide plenty of natural light. By placing the windows high, wall space is maximized.

Solid lumber is stored near the jointer-planer-mortiser. The lumber rack is composed of steel pipe placed in holes bored through the plywood wall and into studs. For strength, the wall has tripled-up studs and is tied into the exterior wall and roof system.

Even stationary machines may be wall-mounted. The compressor rests on a platform above the bench grinder.

Plywood is stored vertically in a rack behind the tablesaw.

A Shop Organized for Efficient Workflow

Store materials near the machines that will be used to cut them. And consider combination machines, such as a jointer-planer-mortiser, to maximize floor space.

16-in. combination jointer-planer-mortiser uses only the floor space of one large machine. Switching between functions takes less than a minute.

I also have a 32-in. bandsaw, a 24-in. thickness sander, a shaper-router table combo, a drill press, and an air compressor. I mounted the air compressor high on a

Get the Most Out of the Available Space

Through his years of experience working in a number of different shops, Day grew accustomed to having separate rooms for machine and benchwork. The partial wall in his shop separates the machine room from the bench room without closing it off entirely and making the modestly sized building feel cramped. That wall also adds significantly to the efficiency of the shop, providing plenty of storage space. Because floor space is always precious, Day went so far as to mount the compressor up high, out of the way, so that the area below could be freed up for a sharpening station.

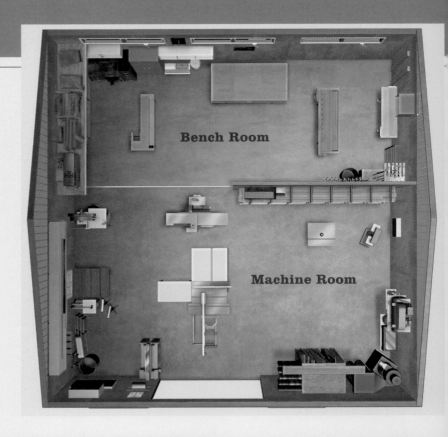

Bench Room

Machine Room

DAY'S FURNITURE REQUIRES a fair amount of handwork. That's why he reserved a generous portion of the shop for benches.

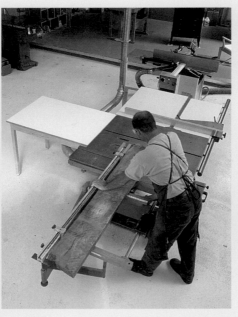

A SLIDING TABLESAW negates the need for a chopsaw station. Sheet goods and solid stock may be crosscut or ripped accurately on a sliding tablesaw.

THE BANDSAW MAY BE PLACED close wall. Leave plenty of room fore and a handle long stock.

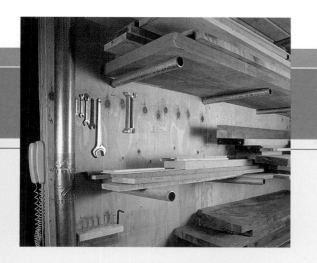

A SIMPLE PIPE RACK FOR LUMBER. Holes drilled into the studs behind the plywood walls anchor the 2-in.-dia. galvanized pipe.

THE AIR COMPRESSOR rests on an industrial-strength shelf along one wall. Below, the floor space is utilized for a more practical application, in this case a sharpening station.

KEEP STOCK AND ACCESSORIES near appropriate machinery. A wall two steps away from the tablesaw holds blades and other accessories. Plywood is also stored near the saw.

wall so that I could use the floor space below for a sharpening station.

Every machine is hooked up to a central cyclone dust-collection unit, which I prefer over portable units that tend to get in the way and take up more floor space. The dust and electrical systems are interconnected through a sensor in the main electric panel. When a machine is turned on, the dust collector starts automatically. All dust-collection hoses and pipes are off the floor, which is safe and makes it much easier to sweep up debris.

To keep cables off the floor, I cut a groove through the floor slab (a very messy task) and buried electrical conduit to reach tools in the center of the room.

A wood floor is a lot easier on the legs and back. It's also a lot kinder on dropped tools. I used pressure-treated 2x4s for the sleepers, then overlaid them with 1⅛-in.-thick tongue-and-groove plywood. Then I sealed and painted the floor with a light gray epoxy floor paint to reflect light to make the room brighter. Crushed walnut shells (available at paint stores) were mixed with the paint to make the floor surface nonskid.

The furniture I build requires a lot of handwork. That's why the bench room takes up half the shop. This room includes two workbenches, hand tools and machines, a 4-ft. by 8-ft. vacuum press, a desk, a sharpening station and plenty of room for assembly.

Electrical Systems Require Careful Thought

While all of the different areas and systems in a shop must be designed to work together to be effective, the electrical system requires as much, if not more, planning. There are many critical things that must be considered. I really underestimated the cost and time involved in wiring my shop.

Plan for all of your current needs and add enough extra capacity for future needs. Do as much work as possible while the walls are still unsheathed. It is much more expensive and time-consuming to add things outside the walls later.

A list of all current and future needs combined with a scale electrical layout of the shop is the best way to start. Obviously, you should check your local code when diving into this area, and don't do anything with which you are uncomfortable or unfamiliar.

I realized my electrical work was more than I could handle alone. Luckily, my friend Roland has a master electrician's license in three states and sunk his teeth into this project. He took my scale electrical-layout sketch and converted it into a workable plan. Among the things he tackled included figuring out the exact panel scheme, phase conversion, and wire and breaker sizes.

Once we were ready to go to work, I ran a lot of the wire and hooked up receptacles while he worked inside the panel, doing the more skilled work. I was amazed at the amount of wire and parts required for the job. The attic space of the shop looked like a spaghetti factory.

Make Sure
There's Plenty of Light

When I was a student at the College of the Redwoods, I loved the quality of light in the shop. It was so open and airy with the combination of natural and artificial light. I vowed that if I ever built my own shop I would try to reproduce those lighting conditions.

For my shop, I had six skylights installed (three in the bench room and three in the machine room) and three wide windows installed across the wall in the bench room. Then I added 8-ft. fluorescent fixtures, flush-mounted to the ceiling, as well as task lighting at the workbenches.

Paint is also an important factor in creating a well-lit area. The ceiling and skylight wells were painted white for maximum light reflection. On a sunny day, I can work by natural light alone, saving on electricity.

Radiant Panels
Heat Efficiently

To work year-round in my shop, I needed to heat it. I settled on radiant electric panels from Solid State Heating Corp. They are compact and lightweight (a 1-in. by 2-ft. by 8-ft. panel weighs about 20 lbs.) and mount directly to the ceiling. They are more efficient than forced-air heat and don't take up floor space.

Buttoning up the shop with proper insulation, weather stripping, and sheathing is important for maximum energy efficiency. I used insulation batts in all exterior walls and wrapped the skylight wells with insulation. The attic has blown-in insulation. All windows and skylights are double-pane, gas-filled, low-E glass. The wood floor in the bench room has rigid-foam insulation between the joists. The side entry door is weather-stripped to help keep out drafts.

The sliding barn doors proved to be a challenge. Because they were both slightly warped, there were gaps of up to 1 in. wide that required sealing. After a lot of scrounging at hardware stores, I figured out the answer: 2½-in.-wide weather stripping designed for the bottom of roll-up garage doors. I tacked the stripping onto the edges of the walls and the header over the doors, overlapping the doors. I also tacked on a strip between the doors.

Stock Is Stored Near
Appropriate Machines

Plan as much storage space into your shop design as possible. It is amazing how fast it fills up. In addition to the cabinets and shelves we all have, here are some other storage solutions I used.

I store sheet goods in a shopmade open-faced plywood cabinet with three compartments. It is only a few steps away from the tablesaw. The sides of the cabinet hold thickness-sander belts, tablesaw blades and tools, and shaper accessories. The top of the cabinet provides more storage space.

Lumber is stored on a pipe rack installed on the machine-room side of the interior wall between the machine and bench rooms. Lumber is heavy, and the storage system must be engineered accordingly. The wall studs are tripled up on 16-in. centers. The wall frame is lag-bolted into an exterior wall stud and tied into the roof trusses with truss clips. The entire framework was then glued, sheathed with ¾-in.-thick CDX plywood and nailed off. Holes were then drilled on 32-in. centers to accept the 2-ft. lengths of 2-in. outside diameter (O.D.) iron pipe. For efficient workflow, the jointer-planer-mortiser is close to the lumber rack.

Various jigs and general storage are in a loft just above one end of the bench room. Because all of the walls were sheathed with plywood instead of drywall, I can drive a screw or nail anywhere I wish to hang a tool or shelf.

My three-phase converter and air compressor are also hung on walls to maximize floor space. My electrician introduced me to an innovative system to support such equipment: B-Line Systems Inc.® manufactures and markets a modular system to support equipment or storage by utilizing metal strut channels with universal attachments.

A Good Plan Ensures Success

Tap the expertise of others when possible. My friends Gary and Robert did the windows and skylights, Richard and Carissa helped with carpentry, and Roland was the electrical mastermind. They helped light the end of the tunnel when it seemed like there was too much to do. With their generous assistance, I now have a shop that is a pleasure to work in.

Paying attention to details while keeping the big picture in mind helps you stay out of hot water. Plan your project as carefully as possible to avoid making major mistakes or oversights, and you'll end up with a shop you are proud of.

ROSS DAY builds custom furniture in Poulsbo, Wash.

Building to Code Requires Some Patience but Brings Peace of Mind

Many small shops aren't built or operated with commercial building and electrical codes in mind. I've worked in some. But for my latest shop, I decided to go by the book. At times this had me ready to pull out what little hair I have left, but I figured it would be worth the headaches in the long run. I didn't want some inspector who happened to drive by one day shutting me down. Trying to satisfy code after the fact could be a nightmare. I wanted to sleep well.

Building to commercial code was expensive and time-consuming. Surveys and site plans had to be created, submitted, and approved; myriad permits procured, and meetings, inspections, and checkoffs scheduled. My dealings with the building and electric departments were reasonably straightforward, though I thought they were overly strict in some areas. All of my hang-ups were through the health department of all places. Go figure.

After this process, I would strongly recommend scheduling a meeting with the supervisor of any department that will affect your project (especially electric). This way you can meet the person face-to-face, discuss the nature of your project, and compile a list of what needs to be inspected.

The city said my shop had to have a separate electric service from the house, which meant having to dig a ditch 100 ft. long and 3 ft. deep. All of the machines had to be on separate breakers, with any wire coming out of the wall encased in dust- and waterproof conduit. All switches and receptacles needed to be dust-proofed. Lights, heat panels, and dust-collection pipes had to be mounted against the ceiling. (The explanation was that nothing should be suspended because dust would collect there and pose a fire hazard.) Home shops and many small, noncode professional shops don't meet many of these requirements.

The city also told me that an exhaust fan had to be hardwired into the wall (no portables), and it had to have enough power to change the air in the shop a minimum of six times a minute. My fan creates a veritable hurricane when I fire it up, but boy does it ventilate! It all seemed like a hassle at times, but now that it's all done, I have a much nicer, safer shop as a result.

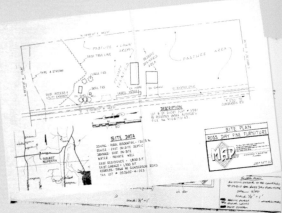

Smart Shop in a One-Car Garage

BY MATTHEW TEAGUE

Tales of bad shops are a woodworker's war stories. After living in five houses in seven years, I have plenty of them to tell: ladders under closeted trapdoors that descended into windowless basements, ceilings that were only an inch taller than I am when I stand barefoot, abandoned radiators, wasp nests, snow, water—good Lord, the water—and a hole in the middle of one shop floor (about 2 ft. in

diameter and 2 ft. deep) just behind the infeed side of my tablesaw. Oh, yes, I could tell you some stories. But that's not my point. My point is that when I moved into a rented house with a one-car garage—9 ft. wide and 18 ft. long—most of my coworkers wondered how I would fit a shop into such a tight space. But after the shops I've endured, I felt like I'd finally arrived.

Thinking Big in a Small Space

Thoughtful layout makes this small shop seem bigger. All of the major machines are stored and fully functional in only 160 sq. ft.

Open storage units are hung high on the walls and outfitted with adjustable dividers.

Worktable with drawers is the same height as the workbench.

Modular construction means the chopsaw station is adjustable should equipment change.

Drill press and grinder are stored below the chopsaw station but are easily removed and clamped to the work surface.

Workbench height allows it to serve as table-saw-outfeed support.

Clamp rack is located behind the worktable.

Essential hand tools are within easy reach above the workbench.

Jigs and fixtures are stored close to the table-saw.

Tablesaw outfeed table doubles as storage unit for portable power tools.

Router table is attached to the left side of the tablesaw.

Small cutoffs are tucked below the switch-breaker box.

Mobile bases allow large tools to be relocated easily.

Planer is stored under the table-saw and out of the way.

Bandsaw can be rolled into open areas to handle large stock.

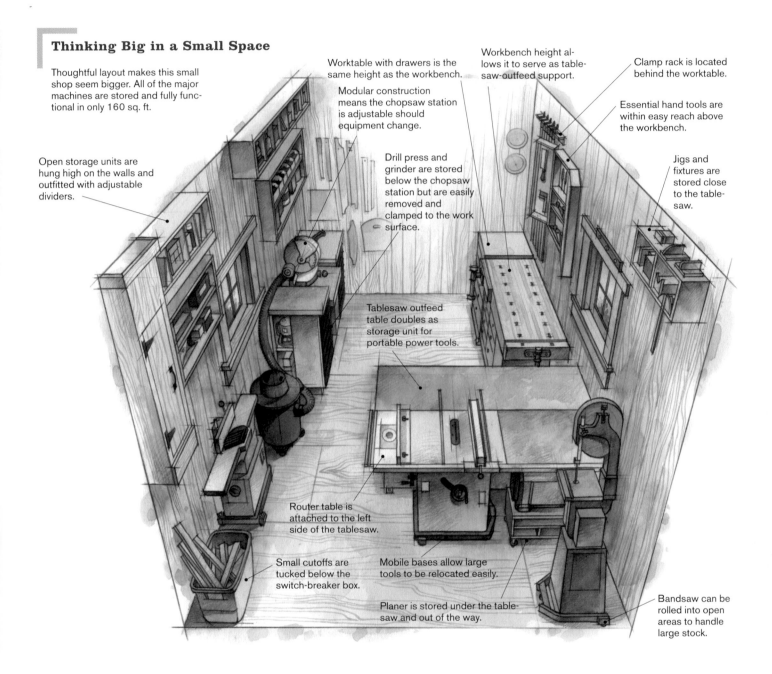

I spent a lot of time planning to condense workspaces and to ensure that machines work efficiently with one another, and I found quick and simple solutions for storage. I think I've turned the 160-sq.-ft. garage into a smoothly running shop; it's just the kind of place where I want to spend a Saturday or unwind after a day at the office. What's more, when I move, the shop can go with me; everything simply lifts off the walls or rolls out the doors.

A Garage Transformed

A few months ago, the garage my shop was to be housed in had bare stud walls and one electrical outlet, stored a motorcycle, and was littered with enough garden tools to dig a new sea. Luckily, my roommate, who owns the house, was amenable to revamping the space, provided that I pitch in with some of the work. He wanted insulated walls, electricity, and wide barn doors on the front—or at least as wide as possible on

Multipurpose Chopsaw Station

This corner of the shop is well thought out and has several uses. The chopsaw station not only provides good outfeed support for the saw, but it also stores the grinder and the drill press and houses two banks of drawers.

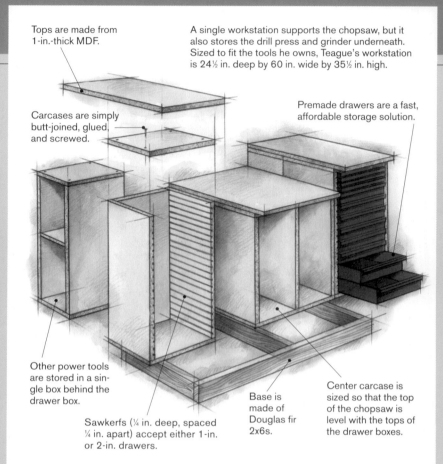

Tops are made from 1-in.-thick MDF.

A single workstation supports the chopsaw, but it also stores the drill press and grinder underneath. Sized to fit the tools he owns, Teague's workstation is 24½ in. deep by 60 in. wide by 35½ in. high.

Carcases are simply butt-joined, glued, and screwed.

Premade drawers are a fast, affordable storage solution.

Other power tools are stored in a single box behind the drawer box.

Sawkerfs (¼ in. deep, spaced ¼ in. apart) accept either 1-in. or 2-in. drawers.

Base is made of Douglas fir 2x6s.

Center carcase is sized so that the top of the chopsaw is level with the tops of the drawer boxes.

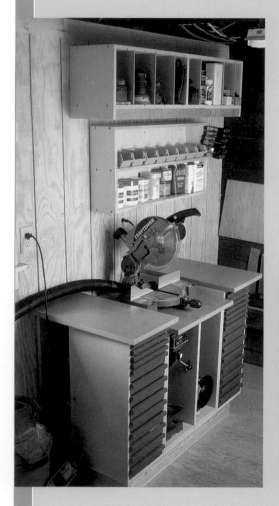

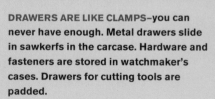

DRAWERS ARE LIKE CLAMPS—you can never have enough. Metal drawers slide in sawkerfs in the carcase. Hardware and fasteners are stored in watchmaker's cases. Drawers for cutting tools are padded.

A PORTABLE WORKSTATION. The drill press and grinder are both stored below the chopsaw but are easily removed and clamped to the work surface.

a 9-ft. run of wall. Renovating the garage would be a hefty task, and I had to do it fast. I had promised my future in-laws a dining set, and if they had to wait much longer, I feared they would take their daughter back.

While I desperately needed a good workspace, I had to remember that I only rent the house. I didn't want my shelving and workstations to be built in. I wanted to be able to lift them off the walls and move them out when I find and buy Connecticut's affordable house. And I didn't want to sink a fortune into cabinets—it's a workshop, after all, and what comes out of the shop is far more important than what goes in. I needed a shop that was well thought out and engineered for a smooth workflow, but not one that was overbuilt. I forgot about all of the garbage that littered the little garage, and started planning on a clean sheet of paper.

Mapping Out the Territory

Fitting the major machines—tablesaw, jointer, planer, bandsaw, router table, drill press, and chopsaw—into a room designed to hold a car (a tiny 1920s Model A, at that) is about as difficult as it sounds. I started on graph paper with paper cutouts of all of my tools. Everything had to be drawn to scale because half a foot in such a tight spot could make or break the shop. As in most shops, large stationary tools are key, but they also demand the most space, so the tablesaw seemed a good place to start.

As soon as I put pencil to paper, I saw that I was going to have to forgo my wide 52-in. Biesemeyer® fence—there simply wasn't room. I downgraded to a shorter fence by changing out the rails, which at this point only meant lopping off the end of my tablesaw cutout with scissors. I soon saw that large tools had to be mobile; if I left open floor space, any tool could be

Workstation Assembles Easily

1 Set the boxes in place. The main carcase is centered on the base and screwed in place.

2 Keep the carcases flush and secure. Clamps hold the drawer box in place while it is screwed to both the base and the center carcase.

3 Exploit every inch. Storage boxes are set behind the drawer boxes and screwed in place.

4 Use a thick top. The 1-in.-thick MDF is coated with a few washcoats of shellac and will stand up to heavy work.

A PLACE FOR EVERYTHING.
Space above the rafters is used for storing–and even drying–lumber.

wouldn't be hindered by workbenches or tabletops. After a few more hours of moving around the cutouts and positioning the major machines, I started thinking about storage space and drawing quick sketches of the outfeed situation. In the end, I came up with an arrangement that housed the major tools in just about 80 sq. ft.—about half the square footage of the entire space. It was time to run electricity and build the walls.

After cleaning the garage of all its old tools and odds and ends, my roommate and I hired an electrician pal to wire the space. We positioned all of the outlets 44 in. up from the floor—just above bench height—and ran them every 4 ft. We also dropped in four 220-volt outlets conveniently located to reach the beefier machines.

We insulated the walls and hung T-111 siding, which is stronger than drywall and does a better job of holding tool cabinets. The light color of the siding opened up the space, and the rough wood surfaces gave the shop a warm, inviting feel. We then built and hung the barn doors, which took only a weekend to accomplish.

The existing wood floor in the garage would have been nice on the feet, but it was too old and uneven to allow my heavy mobile tools to move easily. We laid down plywood flooring over the existing wood floor and covered it with a few coats of water-based polyurethane.

I have to admit I was shocked that everything worked just as it had on paper. Now I was ready to roll in the machines.

Large Tools Rest on Mobile Bases

My tablesaw sits approximately 4 ft. inside the barn doors, leaving enough space on the left side of the saw for my jointer to stand against the opposite wall. And because I put the jointer on a mobile base, I can move it around if I need to joint especially long boards. My small lunchbox planer, which always has worked wonderfully for

pulled out easily and put to use. There still were a few wrinkles—like where my router table would go and how I could consolidate my grinder, chopsaw, and drill press into one smooth-running workstation—but after a little thinking and shopping around, I solved those problems, too.

I also kept an eye on the horizontal arrangement of tools and workstations, making sure that the outfeed from certain tools—like my tablesaw and jointer—

me, was relegated to the cubbyhole below the right-hand side of my tablesaw. It saves floor space, but because the planer is light and kept on a shopmade mobile base, its usefulness is not limited.

One big hiccup always had been my router table. It made sense to save space by housing the router table in the tablesaw, but most models mount on the right side of the saw—a setup I'd never been happy with. And with the right side of the saw against the wall, where it clearly had to go, I couldn't stand in front of the fence when routing—doing otherwise always had seemed unsafe. Still, a stand-alone router table was going to take up more room than I had to spare. Browsing through catalogs and the Internet, I found what is the only left-mounted router table that I know of; it's made by Bench Dog Tools®. Although my choice meant losing 3 in. between the tablesaw and the jointer, I still had plenty of working space. Plus, I was able to get rid of my free-standing router table altogether.

The left-mounted router table works great now, but because my tablesaw table is larger than average—even for a cabinet saw—I had to redrill a few holes in the top of the tablesaw and install spacer blocks to make the router table fit. But the afternoon's

Have Wheels, Will Travel

Machines that have wheels are always helpful in the shop, to be moved to make more room when needed. Modifying machine setup by adding a base with wheels is also helpful.

BUY A MOBILE BASE. Storing the bandsaw and jointer on mobile bases allows Teague to pull them out into the open when he has to handle especially long stock.

. . . OR MAKE ONE YOURSELF. Teague's planer base is nothing more than an MDF box with locking casters screwed to the bottom, and it includes shelves as well.

One Table, Many Uses

The outfeed table not only provides support for the tablesaw, but it also stores power tools and other materials. The shop vacuum can be used for dust collection at the tablesaw. The 1-in.-thick MDF top also serves as a sturdy work surface for assembly. Lag bolts in the base make it easy to level the table.

CONDENSE WORK AREAS. A router table that mounts on the left side of the tablesaw saves valuable floor space and still leaves plenty of room for moving around.

work has proved well worth it. Not only does the table save space, but it also works better than any free-standing router table I've ever had. I dropped in a router lift to make it even more user friendly. Now I can change router bits topside with a quick-action wrench, saving both time and hassle.

As planned, the bandsaw rolled into the front corner of my shop, just behind the tablesaw. It is close enough to the doors that I am able to roll it out and use the open doorway as outfeed space as needed. But

this is only in a pinch. For most of my woodworking—chairs, small tables, and chests of drawers—the bandsaw has plenty of room just where it is.

This arrangement took care of the major stationary tools, and I still had two long walls for the chopsaw station and the workbench. I ended up designing and building a modular chopsaw station that houses not only my chopsaw but also my drill press and grinder. It holds a bank of ready-made

Harry and I have more than 40 years of woodworking experience between us. We started our partnership in 1995 in a leased space in downtown Fort Bragg, California. We ran that shop for five years, renting bench space to four other woodworkers. It got to be a very busy place, and Harry and I spent little time making furniture. We decided to sell the place and build a perfect shop just for the two of us, leaving the landlord hassle behind.

This new shop is a unique and functional workspace (see the floor plan on the facing page). It comes very close to fulfilling our vision of the perfect shop.

Learning from Our Old Shops

Years ago, I had my first shop in Florida in a corner of a storage building that was used primarily to shelter a boat. The space was cramped and dirty and left little room to work. Next came a garage with an awning that enabled me to move my work outside on good days. Harry also had some sorry shop spaces, the most notable being an un-heated space in Minnesota.

The common denominator of all those shops? None of them were designed for, or dedicated to, woodworking. We made buildings into woodworking shops rather than designed a shop just for woodworking.

Our ideal shop would have plenty of natural light, easy access for large pieces of lumber and sheet goods to be brought in, appropriate wiring for three-phase and single-phase machines, and, finally, a comfortable floor.

As Harry and I sat down to plan our new shop, we knew we wanted to build a woodworking space from the ground up.

The Building Blends with the Site

Harry and his wife, Scotty Lyons, own a forested five-acre site about a mile from downtown Fort Bragg, and we decided to build there. We sited the shop to appear as if it were emerging from the woods. Warm and inviting, the building fits naturally into the surrounding redwood forest.

The exterior is typical of Mendocino County barns. The footprint is 60 ft. by 50 ft., which includes a 10-ft. by 60-ft. unenclosed extension on the south side. Harry's wife has a weaving studio in the upstairs portion of the shop, which is about 650 sq. ft. The basic shell of the building was erected by a contractor who specializes in agricultural and warehouse construction. Harry and I installed the windows and finished the interior, including building the second floor and all of the walls. Harry is also a general contractor, and his skills and knowledge made this work go smoothly.

The unenclosed storage area runs the full length of the building. Eventually, we'd like to enclose this area, but for now it's where we keep rough lumber as well as our panel saw for cutting large sheet materials.

The shop's exterior is redwood board and batten, and the roof is steel painted dark green. Sixteen skylights pierce the roof and produce a strong, diffuse light through the interior.

Separating Bench and Machine Rooms

One major influence on our shop's design was the shop at the College of the Red-woods, which we both attended. The shop boasts separate bench and machine rooms. The advantage of this setup is that noise and dust are confined to the machine room, leaving the bench room as a quiet retreat for more intense work. The wall between these rooms has a layer of insulation and sound channel to help keep things quiet. While one of us is working stock in the machine room, the other can be cutting dovetails or drawing in the bench room. Neither disturbs the other.

Harry's Bench Space

Harry Van Ornum's furniture requires a lot of handwork, and he does most of his work at his bench. He keeps frequently used tools nearby, such as clamps, squares, and planes. He admits that he has more planes than he uses, but as a collector as well as a user, he sees them as functional art.

CUTTING TOOLS IN LINE. On his other bench (across from the planes), Van Ornum keeps his chisels and carving gouges within easy reach.

Les's Bench Space

Cizek's fiery-faced tool cabinet in the background is typical of his finishing style, which frequently incorporates bright colors. His work area has the requisite shaping tools and a workbench.

KEEPING THOSE SMALL PARTS ORGANIZED. Cizek made a library card catalog-style chest for screws, hardwares, and other items.

A TEMPLE FOR TOOLS. Cizek decided that his prized, and much-used, custom Japanese spokeshaves needed to have their own home.

The Machine Room

A ll of the tools in the machine room are placed in order of usage for most projects. The setup creates a smooth workflow environment.

DUST COLLECTION FOR LARGE MACHINES. The 36-in. bandsaw and sliding tablesaw are grouped together so that they can share a duct for efficient dust collection.

Workshop Zones

Each operation has a zone within the shop at Four Sisters Woodworking. Lumber enters through the large garage-style door and then makes its way through milling, shaping, and eventually to the bench room for handwork and finishing.

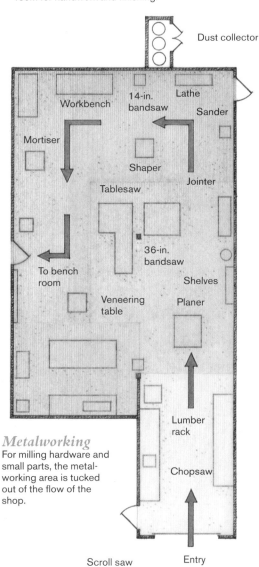

Dust collector

Workbench

14-in. bandsaw

Lathe

Sander

Mortiser

Shaper

Jointer

Tablesaw

To bench room

36-in. bandsaw

Shelves

Veneering table

Planer

Lumber rack

Chopsaw

Scroll saw

Entry

Final shaping
On a path toward the bench room, the shaping machines line the edges of the room.

Milling
Machines are grouped together for easy transition between tasks.

Metalworking
For milling hardware and small parts, the metalworking area is tucked out of the flow of the shop.

Rough Dimensioning
Lumber enters through a wide garage door, is stored on a rack, and is cut to length when needed.

ROUGH LUMBER ENTERS HERE. The lumber rack is close to the chopsaw. The jointer and planer are stationed just beyond.

The 12-ft. by 60-ft. bench room occupies the north side of the building. It is lit by six skylights, five north-facing windows, and three metal halide lamps. Because we spend most of our time in the bench room, we tried to make it comfortable with lots of colors, painted wood floors, and framed prints on the walls. We have found that being surrounded by color and art influences the creative process in each of us.

Likewise, the number of windows adds to the pleasing atmosphere. Whimsically shaped, recycled windows let in light between the rooms and break the expanse of large, white wall.

The machine room is accessed through a 3½-ft.-wide, two-way swinging door. The floor is a concrete slab painted with a durable epoxy paint. We left plenty of room around each machine to make the movement of stock easier. The machine room is lit by a combination of fluorescent lights and 10 skylights. With the skylights, we don't have to turn on the fluorescents until the evening.

Here on the north coast of California, summertime highs reach only the 60s and winters can be cold and damp. So we installed radiant heat under the floor in the bench room and placed forced-air propane heaters in the machine room.

How the Shop Works

In the machine room, we designed our shop around the flow of rough lumber to finished furniture. On the right side of the shop through a large garage door, we unload our lumber to the storage rack. We currently have a small lumber-storage rack where we keep a collection of furniture-grade wood (we keep a large cache in a barn at Harry's house). From there, we can take the lumber directly to the planer for milling. The jointer and large bandsaw are beyond the planer for further dimensioning. Next to the bandsaw, we have a sliding

While one of us is working stock in the machine room, the other can be cutting dovetails or drawing in the bench room. Neither disturbs the other.

tablesaw for sheet goods and other uses. On the perimeter, we've located the shaping tools, such as a lathe, shaper, and sanding machines, because they are used primarily with smaller pieces and don't require the room needed for manipulating large lumber. But we've left plenty of space between machines so that we can move around easily.

Harry and I do a lot of veneering, so we set up the bandsaw, jointer, and veneering table for this process. We placed the jointer next to the large bandsaw because while we're cutting veneers, we often like to joint a face in order to get a clean cut.

We also have a metalworking area where we mill custom parts and hardware. We tucked this part of the shop into a corner of the machine room to keep metal filings away from lumber.

Our central dust-collection system is a three-phase, 7½-hp unit. We routed the

ducting to each machine. The dust collector is outside the shop on the east side to minimize noise.

Each of our bench spaces reflects our personal interest. I use a wide variety of finishes, including aniline dyes, so my tool cabinet has a fiery red face. I also have a cabinet full of my most-used finishing supplies and I am able to get what I need easily. In addition, I have the hand tools that I require, but not much more. I do have a special set of Japanese spokeshaves that were custom made. To honor them as well as their maker, I built a small wall-hung pagoda that houses them.

Harry is a collector and user of old tools, so around his bench he has a variety of classic, old planes. He also is an accomplished carver; therefore, his gouges and chisels are laid out in a line for easy access.

In addition to the natural and artificial light overhead, we installed spotlights at our work areas. We do all of our finishing at our benches. Because we use mostly rub-on finishes, we have no need for a spray booth, and the bench room is adequate for this work.

For the most part, this shop fulfills our dreams. While we wouldn't say that it has changed our furniture, a pleasant shop does make it easier to create quality work. In fact, we believe that our design of a large, open, and light-filled space reflects the philosophy of our shop motto: *Sat cito, si sat bene* (Soon enough, if done well). If we were to start over, the only thing we'd change, believe it or not, is to make the shop larger.

LES CIZEK builds custom furniture in Fort Bragg, Calif. His wife, Norma Watkins, assisted with the article.

A COLORFUL CLAMP RACK. The colors throughout the shop brighten the environment. The clamp rack also provides a reliable spot for storing essential tools. Portholes in the swinging door between bench and machine rooms help avoid head-on collisions.

My Five Essential Power Tools

BY GARY ROGOWSKI

O ne of the few things woodworkers agree on is that we love tools. It is this love that got many of us hooked on woodworking in the first place. We also need good tools so that we can do good work. From this benign and congenial starting point, all hell breaks loose. It seems as if everyone has the correct opinion about which tools to have in the shop, their type,

their capacity, and, above all, in what order to buy them.

Leaving aside the important and absolutely essential world of hand tools, let me venture into these dragon-filled waters with my opinions about power tools and how best to outfit a shop step by step. I can't speak to every situation or shop environment, but I can offer my perspective on how I'd buy machines if I had to start all over again. This article will help you figure out the tasks that are most important and which machines will help you accomplish these jobs.

Never Go Shopping without a List

Tools are not bought the same way as groceries. You don't load up your shopping cart with some tools you need, a few items on sale, and a couple of impulse buys on your way out. You don't put one tool back because it's too expensive and get the cheaper version so you can afford another cheap tool in the next aisle. You don't let tools just

fall into your basket as you head to the checkout counter. Or do you?

Many woodworkers don't consider how the tools might fit into the grand scheme of their woodshop and the kind of woodworking they'd like to do. Your projects will go a long way toward determining your choice of equipment and vice versa. When I started out, I had only a radial-arm saw. Consequently, all of my work consisted of very precise dadoes. I wanted to build secretaries and armoires, but all I could push out of my shop were bookshelves and plant stands. Experience will play a major role in your accumulation of machines and

1. Bandsaw

A bandsaw can be fitted with a good fence for accurate ripping and resawing, and merely by changing blades, you can change jobs from sawing up small logs to cutting delicate inlay.

NO JIG IS NECESSARY. When using a bandsaw, the fence acts as a tenoning jig. Doing this on a tablesaw requires a special jig.

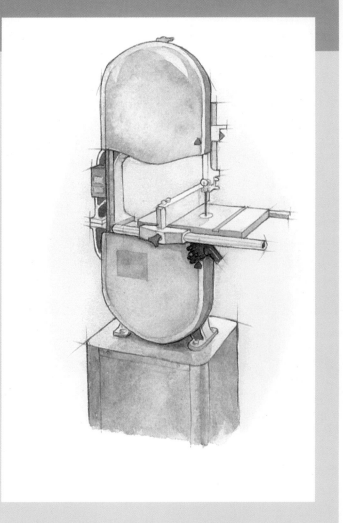

2. Jointer

The jointer can flatten a face or edge to begin the milling process.

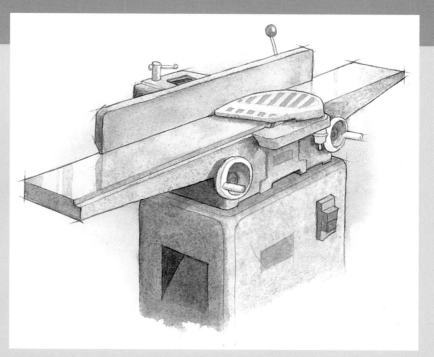

JOINTING A BOARD. Rogowski first establishes a clean face along one edge of the board. After ripping the board to width on the bandsaw, he face-joints the board.

the projects you take on, but keep in mind where you'd like your woodwork to be going so that you can plan your tool purchases.

Also, if your intent is to build furniture and not just to collect machinery, buy your tools as if they're the last ones you'll ever buy. Looking around my shop, it is the economies that I now regret, not the extravagances. Buy your tools one at a time and take a while to learn each of their habits. Try to develop the patience that will also serve you well as a furniture maker and slowly develop your skills with each machine. You may not be able to build that armoire right off the bat, but you will develop solid woodworking skills.

Your First Machine Should Be a Bandsaw

In most cabinet shops, where the work is mostly straight-lined and rectilinear, the maypole around which every other tool dances is the tablesaw. It's also the first big machine purchase for most woodworkers. If you want to build cabinets, your first purchase should be a tablesaw.

But the choice of a first machine must, in my mind, offer greater flexibility than this. There isn't one woodworker out of 10 or one machine manufacturer out of 100 that will agree with me on this, but I think your first machine should be a bandsaw. It is the most important power tool in my shop. I can do more work of a greater variety with the bandsaw than with any other two machines combined.

3. Router

With jigs or fences, a router can cut tapers, circles, ovals, squares, rectangles, and recesses or inlay.

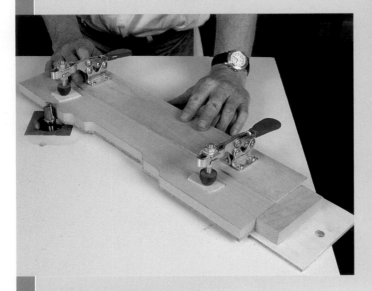

NO NEED FOR A DADO BLADE. A router guided by a straightedge clamped to the workpiece (above) cuts a neater dado than a dado blade and with less danger.

USING A TEMPLATE. A straight bit with a bearing guide can transfer the pattern to a workpiece (above). Mounting the router under a table provides greater stability.

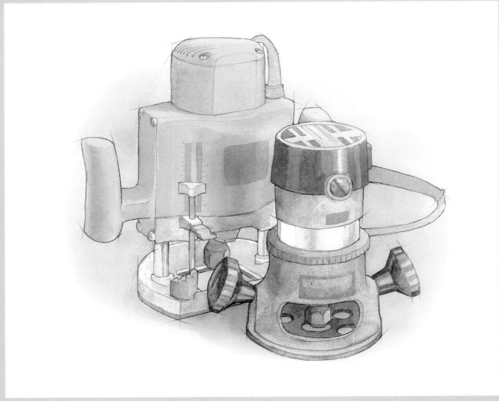

A bandsaw can start the rough milling: slabbing out boards from logs, roughing out bowl blanks, trimming out shapes for carved work, ripping boards to thickness and width, and resawing. The saw will then cover your joinery needs: cutting tenons, finger joints, slot mortise and tenons, slot dovetails, half-lap joints, and through-dovetails. Finally, the bandsaw can also be used for shaping, tapering, cutting circles, curves and templates, edge work, and trimming joints.

All of this work is done with greater safety and ease, less waste, and a lot less dust than with a tablesaw. There is no danger of kickback from a blade because all of the force is down into the table, not coming at you. Even if a board closes up as it's being ripped, the blade is too narrow for the board to pinch it. This narrow kerf also means that a lot less wood gets lost to a cut than on a tablesaw. A bandsaw can be fitted with a good fence for accurate ripping and resawing, and merely by changing blades, you can change jobs from sawing up small logs to cutting delicate inlay.

Now this presumes that you're using a bandsaw with some real weight and well-balanced wheels, with a cast-iron table that is well supported and has a good fence. If not, you'll be frustrated by the cheap piece of sheet metal that is masquerading as a bandsaw. This also presumes that you're building most of your pieces in solid wood. If you're going to be using strictly plywood, buy a tablesaw and a router.

4. Compound-Miter Saw

Put a compound-miter saw close to your bench, and you can nip off the ends of a thousand different boards for projects that pass across the bench.

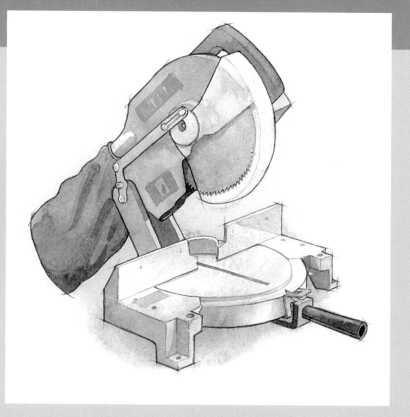

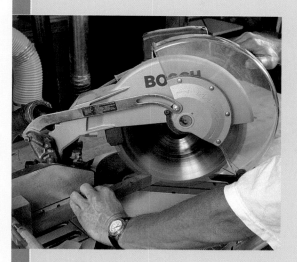

MITERS ARE EASY. With a stop block clamped to the fence, a miter can be cut at the correct angle and location.

The Next Four Tools Cover Milling and Joinery

The second machine is actually tougher to choose than the first. Do you want to be able to crosscut perfectly to length, or do you need a quicker way to mill lumber? The answer partly depends on whether you can sharpen and use a handplane or whether it is just a nice idea up there in the tool cabinet.

A Handplane Is No Substitute for the Jointer If you can't use a handplane fluently, the ability to put a straight edge or face on a board is your next big challenge. Getting wood flat is so crucial when building furniture that your next tool purchase should be a jointer. Even if you are an accomplished handplane user—and I use mine daily—I still wouldn't make someone flatten all of his or her lumber by hand.

The jointer can flatten a face or edge to begin the milling process. From there you can resaw or rip to thickness or width on the bandsaw. The tool does only this one job. It will not plane faces or edges perfectly parallel. But it is such a time- and sweat saver that I think it is worth a spot on your shop floor sooner rather than later.

The Router: Versatile and Portable Your next tool purchase should be a router. You can use one to cut pieces exactly to length, running it topside against a straightedge. Put a fence on one, and you can cut rabbets, tongues, and dadoes for cabinetry. Use that same fence to cut mortises and tenons. With a flush-trimming bit, you can shape pieces to match templates or use router jigs to cut dovetail and finger joints. With jigs or fences, a router can cut tapers, circles, ovals, squares, rectangles, and recesses for inlay. All of this is done with the router above the workpiece.

Buy an extra base for a fixed-base router and mount it under a flat table, and you have a router table. On this you can cut

even more joints, stopped or through, on almost any size piece of wood. You can pass small pieces held in jigs safely past the bit. With a good fence and an efficient dust port, your accuracy and dust problems are solved. A simple setup will turn the router table into an edge jointer. You can template-rout safely and accurately and put decorative edges on boards just by changing bits. There are few jobs a router cannot handle with the simple addition of a jig or a fixture to guide it properly.

A Good Compound-Miter Saw Comes Next The ability to crosscut exactly to length is a time-saver. So the next tool you need to buy is a good compound-miter saw. Notice that I said *good*. Don't waste your money on a lightweight, throw-in-the-back-of-your-pickup chopsaw. Get one that can cut accurately and repeatedly to length. Put it close to your bench, and you can nip off the ends of a thousand different boards for projects that pass across the bench. I didn't have one for the first 25 years in the shop, an absence I regret each time I now use mine.

The Drill Press in the Corner Is Often Underused Because joinery is so important in furniture making, the next tool is another joinery tool: the drill press. It is such a basic machine that it is often overlooked, but the ability to drill accurate holes is essential for making jigs or joints. You can cut mortises on the drill press, drill a series of holes parallel to an edge for shelving support pins, drill for dowel joints, countersink for plugs, or drill for screws. You can also make templates or any of a hundred other little jobs that are just too hard to do accurately with a handheld power drill.

The Remaining Tools Can Wait

I would have to include the tablesaw in this list eventually. I like mine, and if all I did was build cabinets, it would be my first purchase. Once you have one, you'll realize how great a tool it is for cutting boards exactly to width and length. It can also cut many joints, from miters to dovetails to tenons. You can shape with it and use it to cut tapers and coves. I use it more than some of my other tools, but I don't think that it's a must-have machine for furniture making. Don't rush out just to have one: You can live surprisingly well without one. When the time comes, have your money saved up and buy a good tablesaw that will last.

Finally, get a planer to finish the chore of milling your lumber flat and with parallel faces. After first using your jointer to flatten a face, you can then run the wood through the planer to finish your milling quickly.

As for the other tools you could acquire, every shop has different needs. Some people need their thickness sander; others would be lost without a biscuit joiner; I personally love my spindle sander. But I think you could do a lot of work with the first five tools I've outlined here, and with time you could fill in the rest. Consider the work you'd like to do most, then buy well and wisely. If you buy top shelf, you won't be disappointed.

GARY ROGOWSKI teaches furniture making at The Northwest Woodworking Studio in Portland, Oregon.

5. Drill Press

The drill press is such a basic machine that it is often overlooked, but the ability to drill accurate holes is essential for making jigs or joints.

PRECISE MORTISING. With the table and fence square to the drill bit and the depth of cut set, mortises can be drilled accurately.

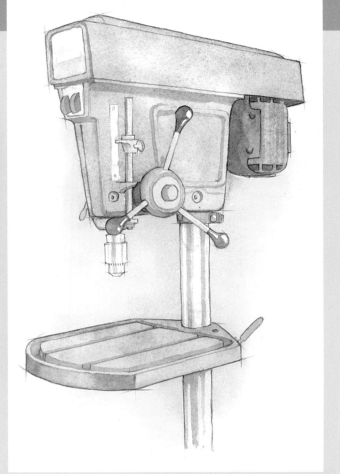

Essential Tools

BY MICHAEL DUNBAR

If I had to guess, I'd say that I own about 350 woodworking tools collected over 27 years. Some work better than others, but at one time or another, I've used them all. In a given week, I probably use three dozen tools. For the novice woodworker, the tool selection in stores and catalogs can seem baffling, confusing, and confounding.

Imagine this: You decide to take up woodworking, and this weekend you are going with checkbook in hand to the woodworking store to buy some tools. Your budget is limited, and you will only be able to buy a half dozen items. Which ones will they be?

First of all, congratulations. Woodworking is a most satisfying pastime, so varied and multifaceted you will never complete the twin processes you have undertaken: acquiring tools and learning how to use them. You have begun a lifetime pursuit. Every journey begins with a first step that determines both your direction and the experiences you will have along the way. Likewise, the tools you bring home are going to influence your approach to woodworking for a long time. You want to choose carefully.

If I had to start over and acquire new tools—what fun!—here's what I'd get first.

Smooth Plane

This is the most versatile of all woodworking planes, if not all woodworking tools. With a smooth plane—most models are 9¾ in. long and are referred to as a No. 4— you can flatten boards. You can thickness and surface wood. You can use it to shape some parts, and it will create some decorative features such as chamfers. Used in conjunction with a simple, shop-built device called a shooting board, a smooth plane will joint edges and square ends. As you progress in woodworking, you will find that one plane is not enough. I have at least two dozen under my workbench of various sizes and configurations.

But before you can use your plane, you have to learn to sharpen it. Sharpening is a gateway through which many woodworkers never pass. In failing to do so, they diminish the pleasure and satisfaction they could receive from their woodworking. They sacrifice efficiency because they cannot quickly do many simple jobs, such as picking up a handplane and trimming a final ¹⁄₆₄ in. from a board. A woodworker who doesn't have a sharp plane is forced to perform an operation like this in complicated and time-consuming ways.

Sharpening is not hard to learn, and it has the added benefit of developing an

understanding of what a sharp edge is and how it cuts. Learn how—there are as many methods as there are planes—and you're on your way to working wood. Trying to be a woodworker without knowing how to sharpen tools is like trying to be a sailor without knowing about the wind; it's almost impossible.

Tablesaw

Like the handplane, a tablesaw is a versatile tool. It performs the obvious tasks of cutting wood to width and length. However, it will also cut some simple joints like miters and rabbets. By using common attachments you can acquire later, like a dado head and a tenoning jig, you can do much more.

Buying and using a tablesaw will help you to resolve the hand-tool versus power-tool dilemma that, unfortunately, divides woodworking into two camps. You do need both. By using your tablesaw, you will discover that the greatest value of machines is their ability to do repetitive labor. But they are more awkward and clumsy than hand tools when trying to do finish work.

You'll find that you work most efficiently when you combine hand tools like the plane with a machine like the tablesaw to quickly produce the parts in your cutting list.

Ruler

It almost goes without saying that wood-working requires measuring. I suggest you begin with a 2-ft. metal ruler. Although you might eventually want a folding wooden rule or a tape measure—you may already own both—a metal ruler is more versatile. Besides measuring, it can be used as a straightedge when laying out work, and that same edge can check boards for flatness and straightness.

Many woodworking mistakes result from incorrect measurements. Learn to recognize by eye increments such as ⅛ in., ¼ in., ½ in., and a full inch. The same holds true for longer increments such as 6 in. and a foot. Twice in a recent Windsor-chair class I taught, students drilling ⅜-in. holes—the bits are marked with a 6 for ⁶⁄₁₆ in.—used the ⁹⁄₁₆-in. bit because they

For the novice woodworker, the tool selection in stores and catalogs can seem baffling, confusing, and confounding.

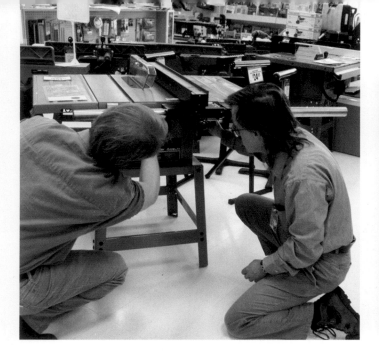

were looking at the 9 upside down. If they had been familiar with basic increments by eye, they would not have made that mistake. Obviously, ⁹⁄₁₆ in. is smaller than ½ in., and ⁹⁄₁₆ in. is larger. My point is that with familiarity, when a measurement is wrong, you will know it intuitively. It will nag at you and demand that you check it again, thus avoiding measurement mistakes.

Mortise Gauge

This simple device lays out mortises and tenons and a variety of other joints used in woodworking. Learning to lay out joints reinforces an understanding of how they work. You develop a sense of what joints work best in certain applications and why.

The fine layout lines made by a mortise gauge bring you close to the wood in two ways: You get close to the wood to see your work, and you get close to the wood as a material. Wood has characteristics—grain, texture, color, hardness, strength—you need to understand if you are going to do fine work.

Set of Chisels

These tools will help shape the mating parts of many woodworking joints and help fit them tightly. Chisels are made in lots of sizes, but to start off, I'd recommend buying chisels in the following sizes: ¼ in., ½ in., ¾ in., and

1 in. Like the plane, chisels require you to learn to sharpen before you can use them. However, unlike the plane, the chisel gives you a close-up, unobstructed view of the wood that's being cut.

Chisels are unique in the way they involve you with the wood.

Dovetail Saw

You will eventually own many types of saws. But beginning with this particular saw will affect your woodworking path. Its purpose is cutting joints, not just dovetails. Using it will not only help you develop an understanding of joinery but also give you a feel for sawing. And after a while, the way you use tools will become automatic. Larger handsaws require more muscle to use, and this overwhelms the tactile feedback. And when you use a power tool, you are as removed from the wood as an astronaut is from the atmosphere. You can concentrate better using a dovetail saw as you work slowly in a controlled manner, making short, easy strokes. With practice and observation, you'll learn all about wood and woodworking: cherry sounds different from pine when it's cut, maple smells different from oak, smooth cedar feels very different from smooth mahogany.

MICHAEL DUNBAR is a contributing editor to *Fine Woodworking* magazine.

Shop Heating Choices

BY KEN TEXTOR

Clouds of breath vapor sometimes obscured my cutting line but never seriously bothered me. Nor did 20 years of wearing long johns and two pair of wool socks significantly slow down productivity in my Maine-based woodworking shop. But the day I picked up some #6 steel screws and they stuck fast to my ungloved fingers, building some sort of heated shop space moved way up on my priority list.

Of course, Yankee frugality was what got me into tundra woodworking in the first place. That wasn't about to change, so I quickly dismissed grandiose plans for a T-shirt-and-jeans-style megashop. Experience had taught me that you can cut, plane, and sand wood just as well at 20°F as at 60°F. But you can't glue, finish, and do intricate woodwork in arctic conditions. Right off the bat, I decided to heat only enough space to allow me to do these warmth-dependent operations, regardless of January's nastiness.

How Much Shop to Heat?

An unwilling student of the energy crises of the 1970s, I knew that choosing a heating source is a secondary question in the winter-warmth game. Minimizing the amount of heat needed was my top priority. With that in mind, the first question was, how big an area do I really need to heat? To generate some dimensions, I started with the assumption that the largest project I would build, and therefore need to maneuver in my new heated shop space, would be something like a custom door. To work comfortably on projects of this scale, I determined that I'd need roughly 160 sq. ft., a relatively modest space.

Because my existing, to-remain-unheated shop already occupied the best solar area, with a southerly exposure and lots of glass for solar gain, I opted for the next-best solar space: the second floor. Because warm air rises, of course, a second-floor location takes advantage of solar gains generated below and avoids the lion's share of dust created on the first floor.

With the second floor ready for insulation, I got a timely and invaluable tip from a delivery-truck driver who had converted his garage into a heated shop. "Don't use fiberglass insulation," he warned. Evidently, the local mouse population had moved into his spun-fiberglass insulation during the first winter. He recommended solid-foam insulation. The 2-in.-thick, 4-ft. by 8-ft. sheets took longer to install than spun-fiberglass batting and cost about $200 more, but I've yet to hear the patter of little feet in my shop walls.

Fuels for Thought

To decide which heating option would be best for me, I began with some thoughts about safety, economy, and simplicity. Immediately, I dismissed wood heat. Although I know woodworkers whose shops have been heated for generations with wood, safety and insurance considerations steered me away from it.

All woodstoves burn with an open fire. In the heating business, an open fire is any combusting fuel that has direct access to air in the space being heated. An open fire spells danger in a woodshop. Even with a so-called airtight woodstove, every time you open the door to feed the fire, the flames have direct access to shop dust and volatile vapors from finishes.

Regardless of the fuel type I chose, I decided that the heating unit's flame had to be completely segregated from the air in the shop.

More than One Way to Heat a Shop

BY MARK VASSALLO

Most of us have a choice about how to heat our workshop, and for those of us in colder climes, the choice can be critical. Three of the four woodworkers whose shop-heating choices are featured here hail from chilly Maine, and the fourth lives so far up a dirt road in Connecticut's rural Litchfield County that he might just as well be from that northeasternmost state.

KEROSENE HEATER

Down the road from L.L. Bean[SM] in Freeport, Maine, Tom McDermott crafts wooden signs in a shop heated with his pride and joy, a Monitor kerosene-fueled, direct-vented heater from Monitor Products, Inc. No bigger than a typical radiator, the 40,000-Btu unit heats the 1,500-sq.-ft. shop, high ceilings and all, for $700 a year. McDermott swears by the Monitor, which has garnered a loyal following in Maine (up the coast in Tenants Harbor, woodworker and *Fine Woodworking*

author John McAlevey is almost reverential about the Monitors that heat his shop and home). The Monitor has a flame that's sealed from inside air; its combustion air is

WARMTH WHERE IT'S NEEDED MOST. Rather than heat his whole shop, the author insulated an area on the second floor just large enough for heat-dependent activities like gluing, finishing, and intricate woodwork. A wall-mounted, direct-vent propane unit does the trick. A propane tank and the small vent hood (by the window) are all you see from the outside.

To my delight, I found that every dealer of every major type of heating fuel was more than willing to pay me a visit and answer all my questions. The cheapest and easiest way to heat a shop, they all agreed, was simply to extend the home's heating capabilities. Many existing oil- or gas-fired home furnaces have enough capacity to heat an additional modest shop space. Baseboard heat is preferable, though, because forced hot air would stir up too much dust. The shop should also be zoned separately from the home, with its own thermostat and an independent draining system. But because my shop was in a building well away from my house, extending my home

brought in from the outside and expelled outside as well. McDermott's unit (its current incarnation, the Monitor 441, costs about $1,500) is fed by gravity from a 250-gal. tank situated outside on a hill above the shop, but in many situations, Monitors can be fed kerosene by an electric lifter pump (as McAlevey can attest).

WOOD-BURNING STOVE

In nearly 20 years of heating his New Gloucester, Maine, shop with a wood-fired stove, FWW Con-

tributing Editor Chris Becksvoort has heard all the arguments against an open flame. Still, he has found that for his shop, a wood-burning stove makes sense. Becksvoort's small Tempwood® heats the 24-ft. by 40-ft. shop without driving him out into the snow, as a larger stove might. Scrap provides about 20% of the firewood. What Becksvoort likes best about his woodstove is the dry heat it throws off, perfect for drying chair parts. Becksvoort feels that so long as he keeps a tidy shop, he need not worry about

safety beyond what is reasonable. He of course exercises common sense: keeping the stove clean, running a dust-collection system that

continued on pp. 66–67

system wasn't feasible. Instead, I considered a number of stand-alone heating units.

Kerosene was at the top of my list because I had heard that the new generation of heaters for this highly refined oil does indeed keep the flame independent of the indoor air. (Older kerosene heaters don't.) New kerosene heaters are also very efficient. But they have one big shortcoming. Most use a fuel-delivery system that depends on gravity. Because I would be building my heated shop on the second floor of my barn, a gravity-fed system was out of the question.

Electricity held some appeal because electric heating units lack a flame and are therefore very safe. Baseboard electricity is an especially safe, easy, and inexpensive means of installing a heating system in a shop. But in many cases, mine included, the local cost of electricity is prohibitive.

Why I Chose Propane

For me, propane was the least expensive and most convenient option. The local sales representative was accustomed to writing up orders for home heaters, however, not for heaters intended for shop use. The first unit he recommended had a flame that we soon discovered was not fully segregated from the indoor air supply. He had to call several heater manufacturers before he could find one that would guarantee the safety of the unit in my proposed shop area. I eventually chose the DV-215-SG Direct Vent Wall Furnace made by Empire Comfort Systems®.

We also had to adjust Btu requirements. The home specifications didn't account for a shop space in which much of the heated air would immediately be vented right back out of the room. (Removing the shop's warm air is necessary when I use some

More than One Way to Heat a Shop

empties into a separate shed, and not keeping a fire burning when he leaves the shop.

RADIANT FLOOR SYSTEM

Although there are commercially manufactured radiant floor systems for most types of new or existing construction, from wood to concrete, Joe Tracy chose to engineer his own system for his new 2,000-sq.-ft. shop on Maine's Mt. Desert Island. He could hardly have come up with a more elegant homemade design in terms of simplicity, cost, adaptability,

ease of installation, and ease of use: 2-in. rigid insulation on grade, a 4-in. concrete slab, 2x6s on edge (to make room for his electrical and dust-extraction systems) and 1⅛-in. particleboard as a finished floor, with inexpensive ½-in. polyethylene pipe running on the slab. To heat the water that runs through the pipe and, in turn, heats the shop, Tracy relies on a standard oil-fired water heater. Tracy was wise enough to consult an in-floor heating specialist for help with details. The system is quick to

heat up, and if Tracy turns it off at four in the afternoon, it keeps heating until six. "It's real simple," Tracy says, "real effective."

types of finishes. The fumes are too flammable and toxic to be allowed to dissipate on their own.) Although a 10,000-Btu heater would otherwise have been adequate for my small, well-insulated space, figuring on increased ventilation, I opted for a 15,000-Btu unit. The larger-output unit cost a little more ($727 fully installed), but it has been well worth the investment.

In the first winter of operation, I kept the thermostat at 50°F when not using the shop space and at 65°F to 70°F when in residence. By the time Mother Nature's spring warmth took over the heating job, I had spent a mere $135 for fuel.

Although there are books filled with specifications for ventilating areas like my heated shop, experience has taught me that there's no substitute for a good respirator. Without exception, I put my mask on every time I open a paint or varnish can.

So while I knew I'd have to ventilate my new space to some extent, I also decided I was not going to try to make the air as clean as a June day under the maple tree. I opted for a blend of mechanical ventilation from a 125-cu.-ft.-per-minute (cfm) fan and natural ventilation from my barn's cupola.

Good ventilation has earned my heated workshop a new nickname: The Men's Room. In the depths of winter, when my cigar-smoking buddies and I need a place to indulge ourselves, my new heated shop fills the bill. A couple of old easy chairs promotes no end of future woodworking ideas. But more important, the heated shop has allowed me to do some of the best and most enjoyable finishing and intricate woodworking I've done in years.

KEN TEXTOR writes, builds furniture, and messes about in boats in Arrowsic, Maine.

Sources

Empire Comfort Systems
Belleville, IL
800-851-3153
www.empirecomfort.com

Monitor Products, Inc.
Princeton, NJ
800-524-1102
www.monitorproducts.com

SSHC, Inc.—Enerjoy Peopleheaters
Old Saybrook, CT
800-544-5182
www.sshcinc.com

* Price Estimates noted are from 1998

RADIANT CEILING PANELS

The electric radiant-heat panels in the finish room above Franklin Nichols' shop in Washington Depot, Conn., are as simple to install and operate as the lights that share the ceiling. After trying every imaginable heating system and finding them all discomforting in the finish room for safety reasons, Nichols hit upon Enerjoy Peopleheaters, manufactured by SSHC, Inc. Nichols figures he pays a little more for electricity, but he has nothing but praise for the five, 1-in.-thick, 4-ft. by 8-ft. panels that heat his cavernous upstairs. Like Tracy's radiant floor, the panels warm people and objects first, keeping materials at a constant working temperature and allowing the air itself to be cooler without a loss of comfort. The electric panels are noncombustible, which gives Nichols peace of mind. The radiant panels heat up quickly, they don't take up floor or wall space, and they're light enough to be lowered closer to you or your work. Peopleheaters are available in panels as small as 1 ft. by 2 ft. The standard bearer, a 2-ft. by 4-ft. panel, costs about $200. Nichols' five much larger panels together cost less than $1,500, a steep discount from full price because they're cosmetic seconds, ideal for a shop and available from SSHC.

MARC VASSALLO is a former associate editor of *Fine Woodworking* magazine.

Lighting for the Workshop

BY JACK L. LINDSEY

The owner of a small shop can seldom justify the services of a lighting design professional. So the task of lighting a shop is usually accomplished by putting up a few fixtures and, if that doesn't work, adding a few more. Sometimes this works, but learning some of the basics about lighting will produce better results faster and more economically in the long run. The most common mistakes are using the wrong type of lamp or fixture, installing too few fixtures, and putting fixtures in the wrong locations.

The first step in lighting a shop is to decide what strategy to use: To light the whole shop in a reasonably uniform manner or to concentrate light at machines and work areas.

For small shops, I recommend uniform lighting because it allows you the freedom

to change the location of machines and workstations within the shop. It also means you can install fluorescent fixtures in continuous rows. This reduces the cost of electrical wiring by allowing you to run wires through the fixtures instead of installing a separate feed to each fixture. If you take this approach, wires are run within 3 in. of the ballast, so you must use wire that is rated for 90°C.

How Many Fixtures Do You Need?

How much light you need depends on the visual difficulty of the work you do and how well your eyes function. Eyesight deteriorates with age, so we need more light as we grow older. Lighting levels are described by a unit of measure called the footcandle (fc). A woodshop should be lit uniformly to a level of 50 fc to 100 fc. You can provide higher levels, if needed, with a separate fixture. Plan for 50 fc if the average worker is less than 40 years of age and doesn't do much work that is difficult to see, such as small, intricate shapes or dark colors. For workers who are more than 40 years of age or who do work that is difficult to see, plan for 100 fc.

Spacing Fixtures Apart As light leaves a fixture and travels to your workbench, it spreads out. You get higher lighting levels near the fixture, with those levels dropping rapidly as the distance from the fixture increases. Because of the diminishing levels of light, you need to limit the maximum spacing between fixtures to avoid dark spots. To figure the maximum spacing between fixtures, you need to know the type of fixtures and the horizontal plane in which visual tasks are performed—for most shops that means the top of the workbench, which is 2½ ft. to 3 ft. off the floor. If fixtures are mounted 10 ft. above the floor and the workbench height is 3 ft., the distance between the fixtures and the workbench is 7 ft.

Fixtures

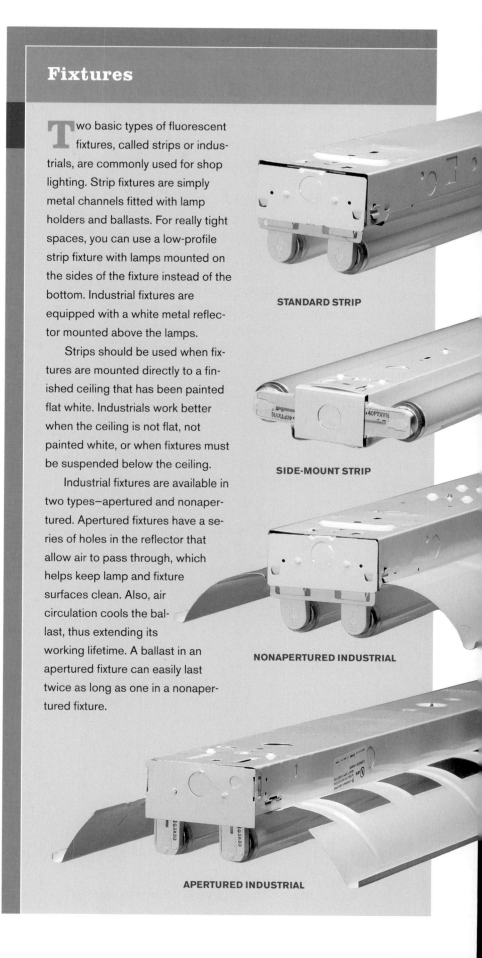

Two basic types of fluorescent fixtures, called strips or industrials, are commonly used for shop lighting. Strip fixtures are simply metal channels fitted with lamp holders and ballasts. For really tight spaces, you can use a low-profile strip fixture with lamps mounted on the sides of the fixture instead of the bottom. Industrial fixtures are equipped with a white metal reflector mounted above the lamps.

Strips should be used when fixtures are mounted directly to a finished ceiling that has been painted flat white. Industrials work better when the ceiling is not flat, not painted white, or when fixtures must be suspended below the ceiling.

Industrial fixtures are available in two types—apertured and nonapertured. Apertured fixtures have a series of holes in the reflector that allow air to pass through, which helps keep lamp and fixture surfaces clean. Also, air circulation cools the ballast, thus extending its working lifetime. A ballast in an apertured fixture can easily last twice as long as one in a nonapertured fixture.

STANDARD STRIP

SIDE-MOUNT STRIP

NONAPERTURED INDUSTRIAL

APERTURED INDUSTRIAL

Placement

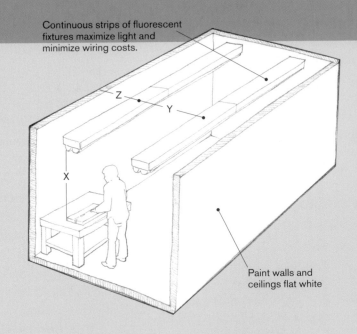

Continuous strips of fluorescent fixtures maximize light and minimize wiring costs.

The older you are and the more detailed the work you do, the more light you need. Concentrated spot or task lighting works, but a uniformly lit space, like the one shown at right, will allow you more flexibility and improve your working environment.

Here are the steps for determining the placement of light fixtures:

1 Measure the distance between the light source and the horizontal work surface (X).

2 The distance between rows of fixtures (Y) should be a maximum of 1½ times the distance X.

3 The distance between a wall and a row of fixtures (Z) should be approximately a third to half the distance Y.

Paint walls and ceilings flat white

Here is a breakdown of how many two-lamp, 8-ft. fluorescent fixtures you will need to light a workshop uniformly to 100 fc of light. For 4-ft. fixtures, just double the numbers in the chart. Consult a qualified electrician to determine the size and number of circuits required to power your lighting needs.

CALCULATING HOW MANY YOU NEED			
Room Size	Energy Saving 60 Watt	Full Wattage 75 Watt	High Output 110 Watt
10 ft. by 20 ft.	5	4	3
20 ft. by 20 ft.	8	7	5
20 ft. by 30 ft.	12	9	8
30 ft. by 30 ft.	17	13	11
30 ft. by 50 ft.	29	23	19

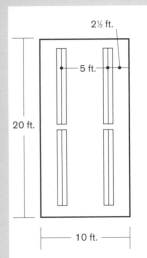

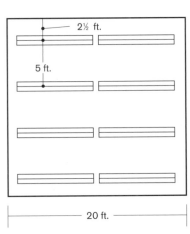

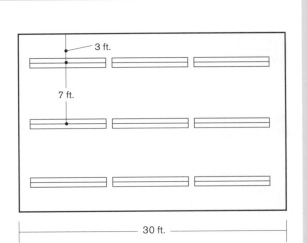

Typical strip fixtures should have a maximum spacing of 1.6 times that distance, or 11.2 ft. Industrial fixtures should not be spaced more than 1.5 times the distance, or 10.5 ft., for that workspace. Changing the fixture mounting height or the work-plane height will change the maximum spacing. Please note that this recommended spacing is not the optimum; it is the maximum. Closer spacing is usually required to achieve desired lighting levels. And remember, walls and ceilings should be painted with a flat white paint whenever possible to reflect light more uniformly around the shop.

Avoiding Dark Shadows Another general rule will help to avoid dark shadows where you least want them: The distance from the wall to a row of fixtures should be one-third to one-half the distance between rows of fixtures, because we often locate equipment and workbenches along walls. See the drawings and the chart at left for more on determining how many fixtures you'll need for a workspace and where to put them. The calculated number of fixtures is seldom a perfect match to the layout of a space, so some juggling may be necessary to fit the fixtures into the room. Don't be afraid to look at alternative layouts before settling on a plan.

Shedding Some Light on Lamps

Fluorescent lamps (see sidebar on p. 72) are best for lighting small shops. The 8-ft. slimline lamp and the 4-ft. F40 are the most common. Both of these lamps are T12 lamps, meaning the thickness is described in eighths of an inch: 1⅝ in., or 1½ in. dia. High-output lamps can be used when higher lighting levels are desired. Smaller T8 (1 in. dia.) lamps are widely used for commercial and industrial lighting, but availability is largely limited to 4-ft. lamps.

Full-Wattage vs. Energy-Saving Lamps

Fluorescent lamps are sensitive to ambient temperature, especially when first turned on, and most lamps are produced in two versions—full wattage and energy saving. All full-wattage lamps start reliably at 50°F or higher when operated on standard magnetic ballasts, and 0°F when operated on low-temperature ballasts. Full-wattage high-output lamps will start as low as -20°F on standard ballasts. All energy-saving lamps are rated to start at temperatures of 60°F or higher regardless of the ballast type. Contrary to what the names seem to imply, full-wattage lamps are actually more energy efficient than their energy-saving counterparts, which save energy by burning less brightly, not by being more efficient. To understand why, a little history may help.

The National Energy Policy Act of 1992 banned the sale of low-cost, full-wattage lamps in most standard colors, such as cool white and warm white, and required that we buy more expensive energy-saving lamps. This was done as an energy-conservation measure, but it created starting problems in cold climate areas. As a result, full-wattage cool-white F40 and 8-ft. high-output lamps have been reintroduced in some areas of the country as cold or low-temperature lamps. Unfortunately, full-wattage cool-white 8-ft. slimline lamps are not available in cold-temperature versions. The only 8-ft. full-wattage slimline lamps available are the high-color rendering types exempted from the Energy Policy Act because of their superior color and premium prices. For example, energy-saving cool-white slimline lamps are available for less than $2 each in case quantities at discount stores such as Costco. Full-wattage, high-color rendering lamps are typically priced at $7 to $9 each.

Lamps

The variety of fluorescent lamps to choose from can make the uninitiated consumer dizzy. Full-wattage 8-ft. slimline lamps draw 75 watts, and the 4-ft. F40s consume 40 watts. Their energy-saving counterparts (labeled by manufacturers with such names as Wattmiser®, Supersaver® and Econ-o-watt®) are rated at 60 watts and 34 watts, respectively. Full-wattage high-output 8-ft. lamps use 110 watts; the 4-ft. versions use 60 watts. To complicate matters more, T12 lamps come with three different styles of bases that must be fitted to matching fixtures.

MATCH THE LAMP BASE TO THE FIXTURE. Fluorescent lamps in all sizes come with a variety of bases to choose from (clockwise from the top): bi-pin, single pin, and recessed double contact.

4-FT. LAMPS   **8-FT. LAMPS**

FULL WATTAGE

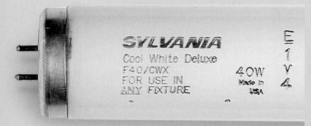

ENERGY SAVING

HIGH OUTPUT

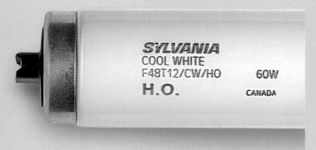

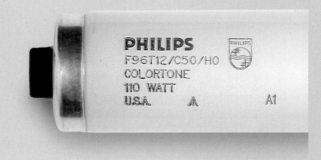

In moderate climates, where temperatures at ceiling level are 60°F or higher, energy-saving lamps are preferred because they're cheaper. But if temperatures are normally lower than that, consider heating the shop before turning on the lights.

Otherwise, you'll have to use the expensive full-wattage, high-color rendering slimline lamps, cold-temperature high-output lamps, or cold-temperature 4-ft. F40s. The drawback to 4-ft. lamps is that twice as many lamps and fixtures are required to light the space, which increases the labor required to install the system.

Lamps Are Rated for Color Fluorescent lamps come in many different colors and prices. Cool white is the most common and is usually the least expensive, and it has a fair color rendering. If you have to use full-wattage slimline lamps because of temperature constraints, consider the high-color rendering type. GE calls these lamps SP, Osram® Sylvania® uses the Designer Series™ designation, and Philips® calls them Ultralume. A numeric suffix describes the visual perception of the warmth or coolness of the lighted space: 3,000 is warm, 3,500 is neutral and 4,100 is cool. Full-wattage deluxe color lamps (such as Cool White Deluxe) are cheaper than high-color rendering lamps, but they are not the best choice for lighting a workshop because they're 25% to 33% less efficient.

If color matching is important in your work, you can buy special Chroma 50 lamps made specifically for this task. But because they are very expensive and less energy efficient, I would restrict their use to an area where color matching is done.

Weighing In on Ballasts

Fluorescent lamps require a ballast to operate. The ballast provides the high voltage needed to start the lamp and the lower voltage required for normal operation.

LET THERE BE LIGHT WHERE IT'S NEEDED. **Even though Lindsey chose a uniformly lit approach for his own shop, he had to fill in some areas with task lighting.**

Ballasts are either magnetic or electronic, with magnetic being more common.

Magnetic ballasts used in fixtures designed for commercial and upper-end residential applications are commercial-grade, transformer types. Almost all 8-ft. fixtures employ this type of ballast. Many 4-ft. fixtures use commercial-grade ballasts, but others contain less expensive residential grades. The commercial versions drive lamps at about 95% of their rated light output. They also contain a capacitor to reduce the amount of current drawn by the ballast and can be identified by their larger size and the letters CBM (certified

Ballasts

When you buy a fluorescent light fixture, you're paying mostly for the ballast. Magnetic ballasts are less expensive and more common than electronic ballast. With magnetic ballasts, you want to ask for a commercial-grade product. Electronic ballasts weigh less and cost about twice as much. All ballasts make noise—some more than others—and they're all rated on the label to indicate how much noise they make. An "A" rating is the quietest. Be certain the specifications on the ballasts match the size and number of the lamps you want to use in the fixture.

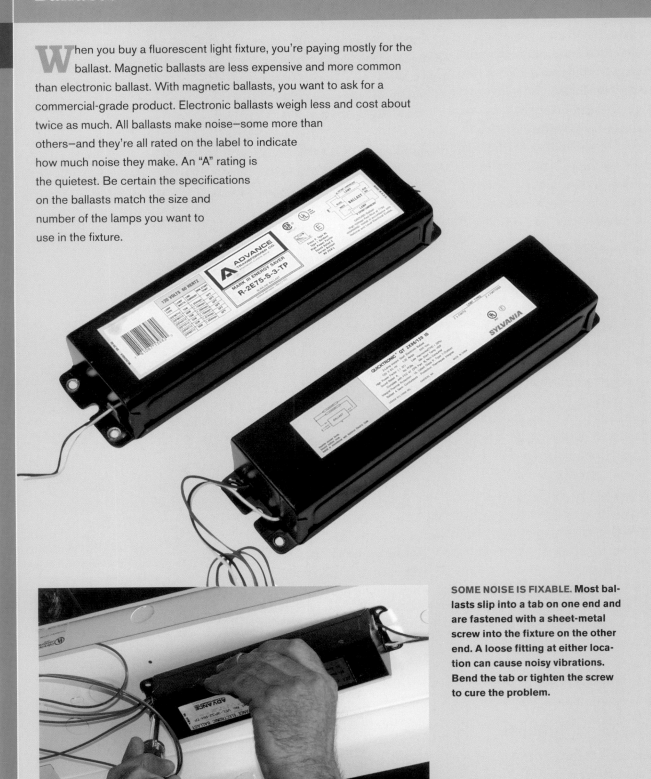

SOME NOISE IS FIXABLE. Most ballasts slip into a tab on one end and are fastened with a sheet-metal screw into the fixture on the other end. A loose fitting at either location can cause noisy vibrations. Bend the tab or tighten the screw to cure the problem.

ballast manufacturer) inside a diamond shape on the label. Residential-grade ballasts produce lower light output, shorten lamp life, and draw more current—all good reasons not to use them.

Some of the 4-ft. shop lights that sell for less than $10 at many retail outlets contain an inexpensive electronic ballast that does not meet the industry standards for commercial ballasts, meaning that lamp life and light output may suffer. But commercial-grade electronic ballasts regulate voltage and current quietly and efficiently, and they seldom produce audible noise.

Magnetic ballasts hum. The bigger the lamp, the more noise the ballast will make. Some hum more than others, and cold temperatures exacerbate the problem. All ballasts have a noise rating printed on the label—an A rating is the quietest. Although

ballasts can be very noisy when they are started in a cold shop, they should be significantly quieter after they warm up. If you hear excessive noise from one or more fixtures, the cause may be a loose mechanical connection between the ballast and the fixture. Most ballasts are installed with one end slipped into mounting tabs and a screw securing the other end. Make sure the tabs and the screw are tight; if not, tighten the connection. If you still find that one ballast is much noisier than the others, replace it. And if the low-level hum that is typical of fluorescent fixtures in a normal operating mode annoys you, consider masking the noise with a fan, a dust filter, or a radio.

JACK LINDSEY retired to the mountains of Oregon in 1996 after a long career as an engineer for the Southern California Edison Co. specializing in commercial and industrial lighting.

Clean Lights Are More Efficient

A little routine maintenance goes a long way toward maximizing the performance of your lighting system. Fixtures and lamps collect dirt and dust, even in the cleanest of shops. A good dust collector and a ceiling-mounted dust filter can't capture all of the dust from woodworking equipment. Dust and dirt on lamps and fixtures can reduce light output by 10% or more during the first year, with additional losses of 5% or more each year after that.

You should clean fixtures and lamps at least once a year to recover this loss. First turn off the power to the fixture. Then remove the lamps, and wash both the lamps and the fixture with a mild solution of water and dishwashing detergent. Rinse with a damp cloth, and dry the surfaces with another clean cloth, or let them air-dry before turning on the power again.

CLEAN LAMPS SHINE BRIGHTER. Dust reduces the light output of fluorescent lamps. Clean them at least annually with a damp cloth and dishwashing detergent.

Low-Cost Shop Floor

BY SCOTT GIBSON

Many a shop is a converted two-car garage built on a concrete slab. I'll say this much for concrete: It's easy to sweep clean. It's also unforgiving. By mid-afternoon, feet hurt. By evening, a dull ache creeps up the back. Tools can be damaged if they're dropped on concrete. And in cold climates, concrete can be a heat sink.

One solution is to install a wood floor directly over the concrete. A wood surface is easier on your feet as well as any tools that roll off the bench. There are other advantages. Electric cable can be routed beneath the floor to power equipment located away from walls. Stationary tools, workbenches, and other fixtures can be screwed down easily. If there is enough headroom, a wood floor can be raised enough to locate dust-collection ducts below. And the cost of material for covering a concrete floor with wood is minimal—about $1.60 per square foot.

However, if a wood floor is going to drop the ceiling height to less than 8 ft., I'd think twice about adding one. But a floor consisting of 2x4 sleepers and ¾-in.-thick plywood is only 2¼ in. thick.

Plywood Floor over Concrete Slab

For a permanent floor, attach 2x4s to the concrete slab, using construction adhesive and powder-actuated nails.

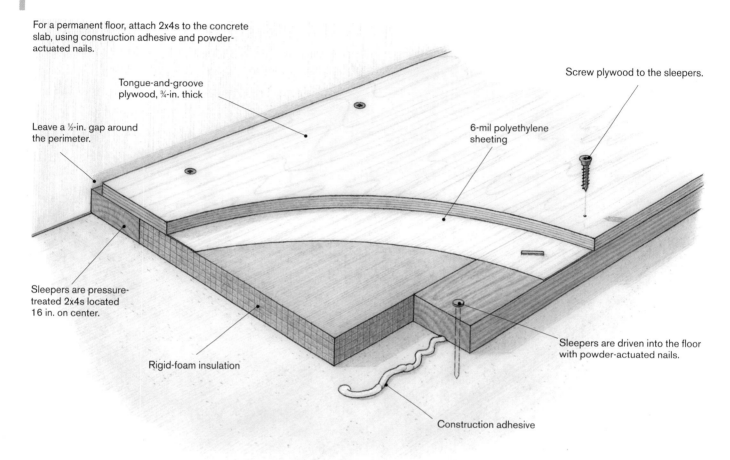

Tongue-and-groove plywood, ¾-in. thick

Leave a ½-in. gap around the perimeter.

Screw plywood to the sleepers.

6-mil polyethylene sheeting

Sleepers are pressure-treated 2x4s located 16 in. on center.

Rigid-foam insulation

Sleepers are driven into the floor with powder-actuated nails.

Construction adhesive

Lay Out the Sleepers First

Because the sleepers will be in direct contact with concrete (for a permanent floor), they should be pressure-treated material rated for ground contact. Concrete can absorb water like a sponge, and untreated wood not only decays but also invites carpenter ants and termites.

Don't forget to wear eye and lung protection when cutting pressure-treated wood and to wear gloves when handling it (splinters are nasty). Even though damp concrete won't degrade pressure-treated material for a long time, serious water problems should be cured before the new floor goes down. In a basement shop, that may mean cutting a trench at the perimeter of the room and installing a subsurface drain system and sump pump. Better to do that now.

Temporary Floor

For a removable floor, leave out the adhesive and fasteners, and place the polyethylene sheeting directly on the concrete. To keep the floor from lifting should it warp, attach a base molding around the perimeter walls.

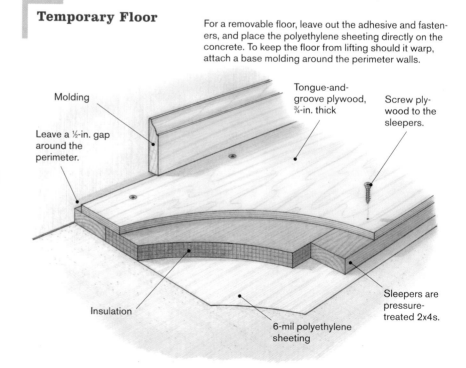

Molding

Leave a ½-in. gap around the perimeter.

Tongue-and-groove plywood, ¾-in. thick

Screw plywood to the sleepers.

Insulation

6-mil polyethylene sheeting

Sleepers are pressure-treated 2x4s.

Sleepers are laid flat, not on edge, over the concrete. They should be spaced 16 in. on center so that the long edges of the plywood always fall on solid wood (see drawings on p. 77). An easy way to get the layout right is to snap chalklines on the concrete to mark the edge of each 2x4. Snap the first line 14¾ in. from the wall, then add 16 in. to each successive line. Sleepers will span minor gaps and voids in the concrete, but serious dips should be filled before installing the floor. Be sure to use a cold chisel to knock off any obstructions that would prevent the sleepers from lying flat.

Once all of the sleepers have been cut to size, place them on or near the layout lines. Then, starting at one end of the room, pick up a sleeper and lay a fat bead of construction adhesive on the floor where the center of the sleeper will fall. Press the sleeper into place. Adhesive alone should hold down the 2x4s, but I recommend using powder-actuated nails, which will ensure that the wood is secure. Powder-actuated nails are inexpensive, and you can find them at a local hardware store. Don't, however, skip the adhesive and rely on powder-actuated fasteners alone. Over time, the floor can wiggle loose. Because the adhesive starts to dry quickly, glue down one sleeper at a time. Remember to leave a ½-in. gap between the walls and perimeter sleepers. In a cold climate, a layer of rigid-foam insulation cut to fit snugly between the 2x4s helps keep out the chill.

Glue and Nail the Sleepers

Construction adhesive and nails provide added holding power. Lay a bead of glue under each sleeper, then nail it to the concrete using a powder-actuated driver.

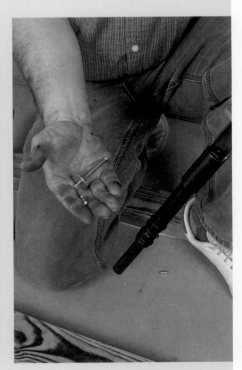

Insulation, Vapor Barrier, then Plywood

INSULATION TO KEEP YOUR TOES WARM. In colder climates, place rigid insulation between the rows of sleepers.

SHEETING PROVIDES A VAPOR BARRIER. Spread 6-mil polyethylene sheeting across the top of the sleepers and insulation. Cover the whole space, and if you need more than one sheet, overlap seams by 6 in.

GET THE FIRST PIECE RIGHT. Take your time placing the first plywood sheet because all of the other pieces will follow its course. Be sure to leave a ½-in. gap at the walls around the perimeter to give the plywood some room to expand.

Concrete: The School of Hard Knocks

Industrial ergonomists—specialists who look for ways to make the workplace more user-friendly—would rather see you work on almost any surface other than plain concrete.

"Concrete floors are a very hard, very dense material. As a result, if you have to stand on them for any length of time, most likely you're going to experience some level of discomfort," said Rob Nerhood director of consultative services for the NC Ergonomics Resource Center in Raleigh, N.C.

Dan McLeod, a consultant in ergonomics in Milford, Pa., said standing on hard surfaces can result in a variety of ailments, including fatigue, stress on the spinal column, and heel spurs. "The latter is more or less a type of tendonitis of the heel," he said, "the symptoms for which are sore heels, particularly in the morning when you first get out of bed."

Adding a floor of 2x4 sleepers and plywood over a concrete slab does provide some relief. But consider also using antifatigue mats. Nerhood said the goal is to provide a material that can be compressed, even slightly, as a buffer between a worker's feet and a hard floor.

Don't overlook your work shoes, either. Insoles can wear out long before the outside of a shoe shows much wear and tear. "If you can't improve the floor," Nerhood said, "improving where your body interacts with the floor at the feet is one of the good steps you can take." No pun intended.

Follow with Plastic Sheeting and Plywood

Once the 2x4s have been anchored to the floor, they should be covered with a layer of 6-mil polyethylene sheeting. The sheeting prevents moisture from migrating up through the floor and protects the plywood from damp air. Overlap any seams by 6 in. and tape them with housewrap tape. If the floor is not to be permanent, omit the adhesive and fasteners and allow the sleepers to float on the concrete. Lay the polyethylene directly over the concrete first, then lay the sleepers on top of the polyethylene (see the bottom drawing on p. 77).

Plywood is next. My first choice would be ¾-in.-thick tongue-and-groove, exterior-grade plywood, but you also can use oriented-strand board (OSB), which is less expensive. Arrange the sheets so that the seams are staggered. That is, start in one corner with a half sheet. On the next course, start with a full sheet. That way, the seams will be staggered 4 ft. apart. The plywood can be nailed to the sleepers, but screws allow you to remove and replace damaged plywood sheets easily. Fasten the plywood every 16 in. with either steel wood screws or drywall screws.

Although plywood is more dimensionally stable than solid wood, it's not a good idea to run the edge of the sheets right up to the wall. Leave a gap of ½ in. all the way around to give the plywood a little breathing room. You can cover the gap with a piece of baseboard or shoe molding.

Finishing the floor is a matter of personal preference. A coat or two of paint or clear finish will help protect the plywood from the inevitable coffee or paint spill. But for a shop, that may be more trouble than it's worth. Your feet, knees, ankle, and back—as well as your edge tools—will be just as happy with an unfinished floor.

SCOTT GIBSON, a contributing editor to *Fine Homebuilding* magazine, lives in Maine.

Four Ways to Control Wood Dust

W ood dust is annoying. Whether you're trying to apply a flawless finish, maintain machinery, or keep your shop fire-safe and clean, sawdust and wood chips are a nuisance. More important, though, is the damage that wood dust can do to your body. Although humans have fairly effective filtering mechanisms in their noses and lungs, the dust present in wood-

shop concentrations (see the photo below) can be toxic, and even carcinogenic. In 1989, the Occupational Safety and Health Administration (OSHA) established industry guidelines for dust. For hardwood and softwood dust, the permissible exposure level (PEL) of respirable dust is 5 mg. per cubic meter of air. The total allowable dust is 15 mg./meter. So what does this mean to the average

BY ALEC WATERS

DEALING WITH TWO KINDS OF DUST. Wood dust can be best handled by breaking it into two components: heavier chips or shavings and finer dust. Hence, the need for two-stage collectors, which settle out larger particles before the air stream enters the impeller to deposit the finer dust into a filter bag. Generally, machines with cutterheads, like this planer, produce more chips, while saws, sanders, and routers produce more dust.

Portable-Planer Chip Collector

BY GEORGE M. FULTON

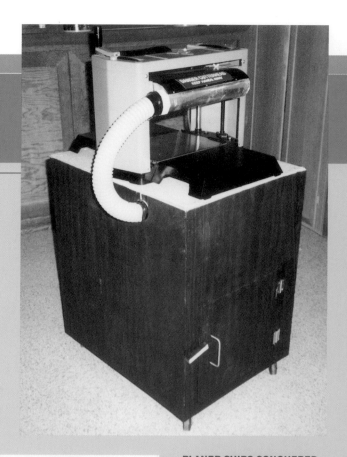

The first time I used my new portable planer, I realized that it needed a chip-collection system. As it was, shavings and dust were streaming out of the discharge chute, floating in the air and settling on my work, the table, the floor, and Goldie, my yellow Labrador retriever, who sleeps nearby.

I decided to make a chip-collector cabinet that would remove dust and serve as the base for the machine. The cabinet had to be compact, connect easily to my Delta planer without substantial modification, and be inexpensive and easy to build. It also had to be stable, like a stand, but mobile so I could wheel the planer out of the way.

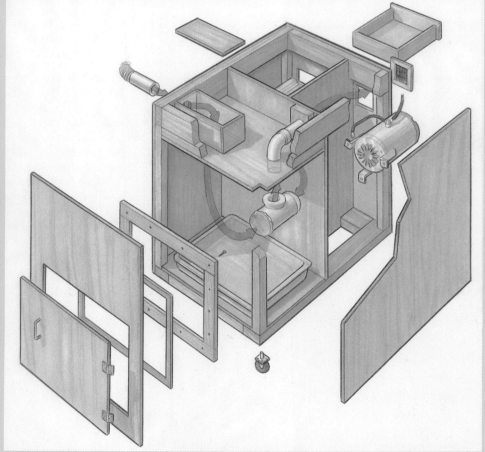

PLANER CHIPS CONQUERED. To tame his biggest chip maker, George Fulton took a discarded vacuum motor and built this combination planer stand and dust cabinet. By attaching a wand to the flexible hose, he can vacuum up leftover dust.

CONSTRUCTION

You should be able to adapt the cabinet to any machine by slightly modifying the dimensions or construction shown in the drawing on the facing page. Basically, the cabinet consists of a frame boxed with plywood, a vacuum compartment and top made of plywood, a discarded vacuum motor, and a plastic cat litter tray. On the infeed side of the cabinet, I mounted a screened vent to cool the motor, and I built a drawer to hold miscellaneous adapters and tools. On the side of the cabinet, I made a vacuum inlet, and on the outfeed end, I added a clean-out door. I fashioned a dust hood (the manufacturer didn't offer one at the time) out of sheet metal, which mounts to the planer and provides a way to connect the dust-inlet hose to the cabinet.

DUST HOOD

I formed the dust hood out of .017-in.-thick (27 gauge) galvanized sheet metal, making sure that the hood wouldn't interfere with the chip deflector or a workpiece. I riveted the hood to the guard, and then I installed 2-in.-dia. flexible hose, which was compatible with the PVC pipe fittings I had. If you want to hook the cabinet up to a standard collector, you'll probably want to use 3- or 4-in. hose and fittings. Because the planer's thicknessing range is achieved by raising and lowering the cutterhead, I used flexible hose. That also lets me easily disconnect it from the hood, pop on a standard vacuum pick-up wand, and clean up dust around the planer.

CABINET

I constructed the frame, as shown in the drawing on the facing page, using 2x4s and 2x2s. For the box sides, top, and vacuum chamber, I used ½-in. and ⅜-in. plywood. To make cleanup easier, I adhered plastic laminate to the cabinet top. I mounted a discarded vacuum-cleaner motor in the exhaust chamber using aluminum angle brackets. I grounded the motor housing using a lug terminal and the green wire of the motor cable. After I installed the vent and drawer on the infeed end, I added a partition between them, so the air is exhausted through the vent and the opening in the floor of the box.

Although the vacuum compartment's seams were tight, I applied a bead of caulk all around the interior corners and inlet box joints. Because the clean-out door had potential to leak air, I surrounded the opening's inner frame with a ¼-in. by ¾-in. weather-seal gasket. A pivoting latch compresses door to gasket.

DUCT WORK

The exhaust duct consists of a pine collar, 2-in. PVC pipe and elbow, and a 4-in. tee. I formed a section of aluminum window screen over the two open ends of the tee and secured them with rubber bands. You could cover the screen with nylon stocking to further filter dust. For the inlet duct, I used 2-in. PVC, flexible hose, and threaded coupling (see photo on facing page).

WIRING AND FINAL DETAILS

To allow the vacuum to run after the planer is off, I installed a toggle switch next to the cutterhead switch and wired it to the motor. After I secured four furniture casters to the bottom frame of the cabinet, I mounted the planer to the cabinet with bolts and T-nuts. Finally, I placed a plastic waste tray in the vacuum chamber under the inlet box to gather the lion's share of shavings.

Now my dog Goldie dozes fairly contentedly, although she is probably wondering if something can be done about all the noise.

GEORGE FULTON is a retired electrical engineer and a hobbyist woodworker in Arnold, Maryland.

Shop Air-Filtration Box

BY JIM WHETSTONE

I was convinced that my shop's exhaust system was not that efficient. I suppose it was removing fumes and radon gas adequately, but I felt it needed to do a better job of removing dust from the air. So I decided to build an air-filtration box. I made it out of plywood, a fan, a timer, and a household furnace filter, which catches the dust. The box hangs from the ceiling: still accessible but out of the way (see the photo at right).

DESIGN AND MATERIALS

For the box, I used about one-quarter of a 4x8 sheet of 3⁄4-in. birch plywood. The fan is a 9-in. axial fan motor ($55) from Grainger^{SM}. I bought a 30-minute mechanical timer (instead of an on/off switch), so I could leave the shop with the fan running. Originally, I used a 12x12 fiberglass furnace filter, which worked okay. But lately, I've been using a finer-mesh synthetic filter, which costs about $1.20. A filter, which arrests 85% of particles in the 3 to 5 micron size, lasts about three weeks if I'm using my machinery heavily. (Be sure to write the installation date on new filters.) I picked up the rest of the hardware and wiring (see the drawing on the facing page) at my hardware store.

When building the box, I called Grainger to see about the fan-spacing requirements. They advised that a 6-in. space between the filter and the fan would be fine. I made the box's top 2¾ in. longer than the box so that I'd have a mounting surface. I routed rabbets to receive the fan mounting piece and the filter. Before I glued up the box, I drilled all its holes, including the ones for the electrical box.

A simple open-panel door holds the filter in place. I used ¾-in. pine for the door's half-lapped frame and to help direct dust into the box, I chamfered the door's inside edges. A pair of small hinges and a hook-and-eye catch secure the door to the box.

On the back of the box, I cut a 9-in.-dia. hole for the fan using my jigsaw. After I screwed the fan to the

READY TO FILTER SHOP AIR. After installing a fine-mesh, filter in his ceiling-hung filtration box, Jim Whetstone can breathe easier. Although he owns a shop vacuum and dust collector already, he wanted additional protection from finer dust. (Photo by Alec Waters, © The Taunton Press, Inc.) w106wa3.fpo

back, I dry-assembled all the parts and turned the unit on. Everything worked properly, so I stripped the hardware, sanded the box, and painted and urethaned it to match my other shop cabinets.

ASSEMBLY AND MOUNTING

When putting the box back together, I added lock washers while mounting the fan to the back. For safety reasons, I sandwiched a piece of ½-in. by ½-in. metal hardware cloth between the fan and plywood. Next I installed the electrical box and wired the timer to the fan. I located the air-filtration box over my bench where there's good head room and a nearby duplex ceiling receptacle. I drilled holes in the box's top 16 in. on center to match my ceiling joist spacing. Finally, I screwed the air-filtration box in place, inserting ¼-in.-thick wood spacers behind the screws, so the unit would hang below the ceiling slightly.

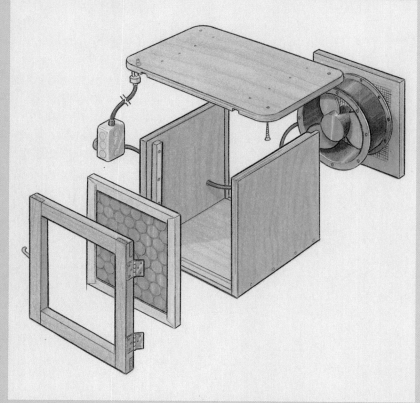

I've been using the 560-cu.-ft.-per-minute filtration box off and on now for a year and have noticed the air is definitely less dusty, though I still use a respirator for certain work. Also, the noise level is quite acceptable (47 dB). I can still hear the radio or television.

JIM WHETSTONE has been working wood in New Cumberland, Pennsylvania, for more than 30 years.

woodworker? It means dust collection and air filtration in the shop are more important now than ever.

Luckily, there are hoards of dust-sucking machines available commercially. For the modest needs of carvers, there are lap-top models. And for the high volumes of dust in production shops, there are cyclone separators. However, for many small-shop owners, the big price tag and size of the manufactured and high-end collectors are deterrents. That's why many woodworkers have come up with their own dust-controlling ideas. Over time, *Fine Woodworking* magazine has gathered an assortment of shopmade systems submitted by readers. Some units are frugally cobbled together from scrapwood and spare parts; others resemble professionally built machines. I've picked out a sampling of units, both simple and involved, to show what home-brewed ingenuity and resourcefulness can yield. But before I share the designs, I'll discuss general dust-handling strategies.

Collectors, Vacuums, and Filters—Oh, My!

Sawdust actually consists of a range of particle sizes. Both single and two-stage dust extractors, so-called source-capture collectors, use impellers (a rotor with fan-like blades) that propel air and dust through ducts to a storage container, usually a bag. But two-stage units take advantage of different particle sizes. They divide heavier chips from lighter dust before the mixture reaches the impeller. The first stage relies on gravity to cause heavier particles to fall into a drop box (usually a barrel or bin). The lighter dust continues on to be collected in the bag. But don't breathe easy yet.

Sources

In-Lap Dust Collection Systems
Racine, WI
414-633-8899

Center for Safety in the Arts
5 Beekman St., Suite 820
New York, NY 10038
212-227-6220
(For a chart of toxic woods, send $2.50.)

John Timby
P.O. Box 1904
Deming, NM 88031
(Write for more on his dust-extraction units.)

Grainger
800-473-3473
(axial fan motor)

American Air Filter Co.
Elizabethtown, PA
717-367-5060
(finer-mesh synthetic filters)

Jack Minassian
15-20 201 St., Bayside, NY 11360
(Send $6 for detailed construction
drawing of his dust-collection box.)

*Note that price estimates are from 1994

Most dust-collection systems capture from 50% to 90% of the dust. Also, the bags themselves catch dust only so fine. As one reader, Daryl Rosenblatt, says: "Dust collection is a philosophy. No single collector will get it all." And it's the tiny particles (those under 10 microns are respirable) that are so damaging when inhaled, especially to those who suffer allergies. Depending on the person, the exposure level, and the wood species, symptoms can range from eye, nasal, and skin irritation to respiratory and cardiac problems. That's where the free-hanging filtration units come into play. Some operate electrostatically (charging the dust particles so they can be removed), and others are fan powered. Both types use filters to manage the dust. But the only sure way to protect your lungs is to use a fresh-air-supplied respirator that has a proper-fitting mask. At the least, you should use a dust mask. In fact, after much tribulation trying to make his home shop dust-free, Rosenblatt now advocates a four-system approach: a dust collector, a shop vacuum, an air-filtration unit, and a respirator.

The shortcomings of conventional dust collectors have prodded other solutions. Because of severe wood allergies, John Timby, a New Mexico woodworker and retired design engineer, developed a two-bag (one is impervious) extraction unit called a "depression chamber" that keeps dust from reentering the shop. It's designed to remove all micron-sized and under particles. Timby also offers a pair of video tapes for $60, which explore this unit and ways to hook up dust collectors to stationary machines.

Designing Your Own System

Now that you know how dust behaves, you have to decide what is best for your shop. When designing a collection system, you will want to properly size its motor (in hp), air-handling rate (in cubic feet per minute), and ductwork (in diameter, length, and junctions) around your machine requirements. Be aware, too, that universal motors, commonly found in vacuums, won't hold up as well as induction motors most often used in commercial dust collectors.

When it's time to build your system, be sure to eliminate fire and other hazards. For example, ground the duct work to dissipate any static charge and try to select an

Dust-Collection Box
BY JACK MINASSIAN

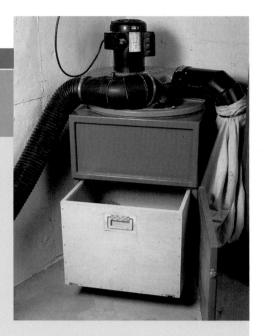

MOBILE BOX IMPROVES COLLECTOR. By replacing his dust collector's 55-gal. drum with a cabinet, Jack Minassian can wheel the unit to any machine in the shop. Opening the door reveals a file-cabinet-like drawer, which can be readily emptied.

I built a dust-collection box to replace the 55-gal. steel drum that my Delta dust-collection unit is designed for. The box has a drawer, which lets me clean out dust without having to remove the heavy motor from the drum. The cabinet is ⅜-in. Baltic-birch plywood with exterior poplar strips that protect the plywood edges and allow easy assembly. The drawer, which has waxed oak runners and guides, is made of ¼-in. plywood.

The photo at right shows how the box is made. Most of it assembles easily, but a few details are worth noting. When cutting the 22-in.-dia. opening in the top, use a sabersaw fitted with a radius strip, and pivot the saw like a compass. The resulting circular cutout can be used as a form for the support ring. I made my 1-in.-wide ring by laminating 7-ft. strips of ³⁄₃₂-in. by 1⅛-in. poplar with scarf-joint ends.

To clamp the ring, I used 16-gauge by ¾-in. nails with square wooden pads

under the heads. To remove the nails, I pried under the pads. Next I placed the ring over the form. Then, using a center pivot and a sanding disk on my tablesaw, I sanded the ring perfectly round. With the blade back in the saw, I held the ring vertical and rotated it to rip the ring to its correct thickness.

The inside of the door has a gasket made of ⅛-in.-thick self-sticking neoprene, which will compress to about ¹⁄₁₆ in. I hung the door on a 1½-in.-wide piano hinge, and then I installed blocks to the cabinet sides to mount two buckle-hasp latches (made by Brainerd Manufacturing Co.®), which are available at most hardware stores.

You can round the edges of the poplar trim, either before or once everything is assembled, using a ¼-in. roundover bit and a router. After you determine the position of your collection unit, shape the support ring for a snug fit. Finish the box as you like (I painted mine Powermatic-machinery

green), and then fasten 2-in., 90-lb. swivel casters to the bottom. Finally, install your collector on top.

JACK MINASSIAN is a retired architect who lives in Bayside, New York.

impeller material that won't conduct sparks. Also, see that bags have adequate capacity, and clean them often, and see that filters are fine mesh, but won't clog. For air-filtration units, avoid creating an airflow pattern that will blow across your face. Finally, make sure that there's enough fresh air coming in the shop to replace what's being exhausted.

Designing your own system—as in the four examples here—quickly leads you to where the dust is collected. In all cases, the units were inexpensive to build using readily available materials like plywood. The first unit is a cabinet that collects dust and chips from the most demanding machine in the shop: the planer (see p. 82). The second is a ceiling-mounted air-filtration box, which hangs out of the way and runs quietly (see p. 84). The

Mobile Stand with Intake Hood

BY GREGOR JAKOB

Sanding dust is an ever-present problem in my woodshop. I've used face masks and left the windows open; then I designed a dust-collector stand that connects to my shop vacuum. The setup works for benchtop sanding (see the photo below) and for my stationary drum sander.

To make the stand, I used plywood, pine, melamine, arborite laminate, and metal stove pipe. The base has casters and a telescoping column, which provides height adjustment. A pivoting oak head allows the funnel-shaped hood to swivel and tilt. The hood's adapter tube fits my 2-in.-dia. vacuum line.

GREGOR JAKOB is a technology teacher in Mississauga, Ontario, Canada.

DUST-REMOVING HELPER. When sanding, Jakob rolls up this hooded stand and connects it to his shop vacuum.

third unit is a portable dust-collection box, which has an easy-to-clean bin and is fed by a standard barrel-top collector (see p. 87). The fourth unit is actually a mobile stand with an adjustable collector hood that is powered by an ordinary shop vacuum (see p. 88). Just like building a furniture project, the nice thing about these shop-built collectors is you can mix and match features to fit your needs. If you're still not happy with the results (or if your spouse incessantly complains of wood dust and noise), you can always go back to making shavings with hand tools.

ALEC WATERS is a former assistant editor of *Fine Woodworking* magazine.

Small-Shop Dust Collectors

BY SANDOR NAGYSZALANCZY

Even woodworkers with no natural housekeeping skills eventually may recognize that the sawdust piling up on the shop floor is a nuisance. Sawdust is also a fire hazard and, worse, poses serious health risks. Some of the bits of dust pumped into the air are many times smaller than the human eye can detect. Dust particles that small can stay aloft for hours, plenty of time to be inhaled and lodge in the deepest cavities of your lungs. Exposure to dust over long periods of time may even give you cancer.

These are good reasons to have a central dust-collection system. A well-designed system whisks wood dust and debris from the machinery, work stations, and floor sweeps to a canister or bag. Good-quality filters capture most of the dust before the air is returned to the shop. Any small particles that sneak through can be controlled with an air-filtration device or by wearing a dust mask. The result is a healthier and cleaner shop.

You can get good results by mounting a collector on a dolly and wheeling it from job to job. But I think a central collection system—consisting of a collector, rigid metal ducts, and flexible hose—is the best approach. A good central collector is tailored to suit the equipment in your shop.

Central Collectors vs. Shop Vacuums

Shop vacuums or small portable collectors work well when collecting dust from a single machine or from portable power tools. But many of them don't have much chip-holding capacity. A shop vacuum has a small universal motor, like those that are used in most portable power tools, running at a high speed to drive a fan that draws sawdust through a 1-in. to 2 ¼-in. flexible hose. Hoses that small can clog easily with large shavings.

A central collector is like a big shop-vacuum cleaner, with some important differences. A central collector employs a powerful induction motor (the kind used in most stationary machines) to drive a large-volume fan. This blower, or impeller, moves chips and sawdust through ductwork 3 in. to 6 in. or more in diameter. A central dust collector moves a large volume of air at 3,500 to 4,000 feet per minute (fpm)—a speed just high enough to keep chips and dust moving through the ducts in a well-designed system.

In contrast, a shop vacuum moves a small volume of air at a high velocity—8,000 fpm or more—through a small-diameter hose. This high-velocity air is subject to more friction, which is why these machines quickly choke if you try to draw sawdust through more than just a few feet of hose.

SINGLE-STAGE COLLECTORS, such as this 2-hp unit, connect easily to small central-collection systems. One drawback is that the debris enters through the unit's blower where cutoffs or stray bits of metal can cause problems.

Single-Stage Collector

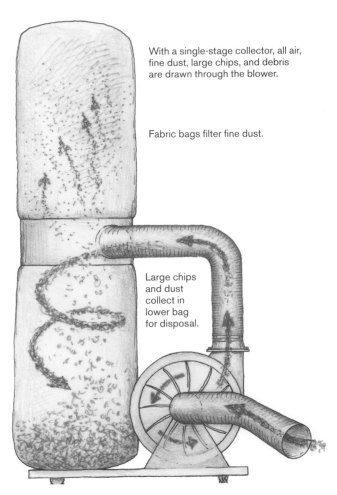

With a single-stage collector, all air, fine dust, large chips, and debris are drawn through the blower.

Fabric bags filter fine dust.

Large chips and dust collect in lower bag for disposal.

Two-Stage Systems Are Safe and Efficient

Once you've decided to buy a central dust collector for your shop, you are faced with a number of choices. The most basic is whether to go with a single-stage or a two-stage design (see drawings below). Prices range from less than $200 for a 1-hp single-stage version to more than $2,500 for a big-capacity two-stage collector.

Single-stage collectors are widely advertised in woodworking-supply catalogs and magazines, and most of them are manufactured in Taiwan. These simple devices consist of a blower and a filter-bag assembly (see the photo on the facing page). Incoming dust and chips travel through the blower and then into fabric bags. The lower bag collects the sawdust.

A two-stage collector removes larger particles and coarse dust before air enters the blower. Most two-stage collectors use either a canister or a cyclone (more about cyclones later) to separate heavier debris. Only fine dust moves through the blower and into the filters.

Two-stage collectors have several advantages over single-stage models. Because large debris doesn't go through the blower, there's less wear and tear on the fan and less racket caused by chunks of wood striking the blower. More important, this reduces the risk of a fire or explosion. Bits of metal, like a nail or a staple, can cause a spark when they hit the blower and ignite dust inside the filter bag. When only very fine dust is sent to the filters, they become more efficient: The filters are less likely to clog, they will need to be cleaned less often, and they will allow air to flow more freely through the system.

Disadvantages? Canister-style collectors and cyclone collectors are more expensive than comparably sized single-stage units, and many two-stage systems are just too big for small shops.

Two-Stage Collector

With a two-stage collector, like the canister style shown here, large chips and debris settle out when air and wood dust enter the canister.

Only fine dust passes through the blower and into the filter bag.

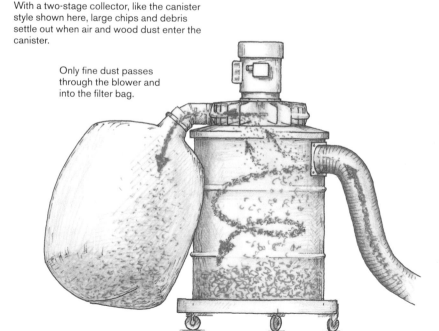

THE LID CAN BE HEAVY with this kind of two-stage collector. One option would be to install a block and tackle nearby with a wall cleat to tie off the rope.

A BUILT-IN CYCLONE does an excellent job separating chips and dust before they reach the blower. This Delta 50-903 collector has a 5-hp motor.

One drawback to canister-style collectors, sometimes called barrel-top collectors, is that you must lift off a heavy top assembly to empty the drum (see the photo on p. 91). You can make that chore easier by hooking a block and tackle to a ceiling joist over the unit to raise and lower the top.

The low cost and availability of single-stage models make them popular in many small woodworking shops. With a pre-separator added in front of the blower, a single-stage collector will perform like a two-stage unit. This conversion will increase the chip-holding capacity of the collector and make sawdust easier to empty. More important, it will allow you to collect larger chips and metal debris more safely.

Cyclones, Separator Cans, and Drop Boxes

A cyclone is one kind of pre-separator. It's a sheet-metal cylinder with a funnel-shaped lower section that empties into a drum. Incoming air full of dust and chips swirls around until the heavier debris slows down and drops to the bottom.

You can purchase a system with a built-in cyclone, such as the Delta 50-900 series (see the left photo above). Or you can build or buy a cyclone and connect it to a single-stage system. Be sure the cyclone fits the air-moving capacity of your blower and ductwork system.

If you can't afford a cyclone, you can add a pre-separator to your system by installing either a dust-separator can or a drop box ahead of the blower. Though they are less efficient than a cyclone, these devices are inexpensive and can increase the chip-holding capacity of your system.

A dust-separator can is a drum or a barrel with an inlet and an outlet arranged so that heavier materials settle out as dust and debris enter it. Only fine dust travels to the blower and the filters.

You can build your own separator can by installing a few plastic plumbing fittings into the removable lid of a fiber or steel drum. Flexible hoses connect the inlet to the ductwork and the exhaust to the blower. Or you can buy a cast-plastic lid that's designed to fit over a standard 30-gal. galvanized-steel trash can (see the photo at right on the facing page). This inexpensive lid accepts 4-in.-dia. hoses and hooks up quickly to most systems. The lid is available through a number of woodworking-supply catalogs.

A drop box is an even more basic pre-separator (see the drawing below). It consists of an airtight plywood box with an inside baffle. As air from the ductwork enters on one side, chips settle and fall into a removable bin inside the box.

Choose a Powerful Collector

To determine the size and power of a central collector, you'll need to know two things: the amount of air the collector's blower is capable of moving, measured in cubic feet per minute (cfm), and the amount of air resistance in the ductwork that the collector must overcome, stated as static pressure (sp). Generally, more motor horsepower and larger blowers mean more air-moving capacity for the collection system.

The amount of power you'll need depends on three factors:

1. How much sawdust your shop produces. The more debris a machine produces, the greater the volume of air needed to capture and convey it. See the chart on p. 95 for average cfm requirements for small-shop machines.

2. How far the ductwork must move sawdust. The farther or more roundabout the distance debris must travel, the stronger

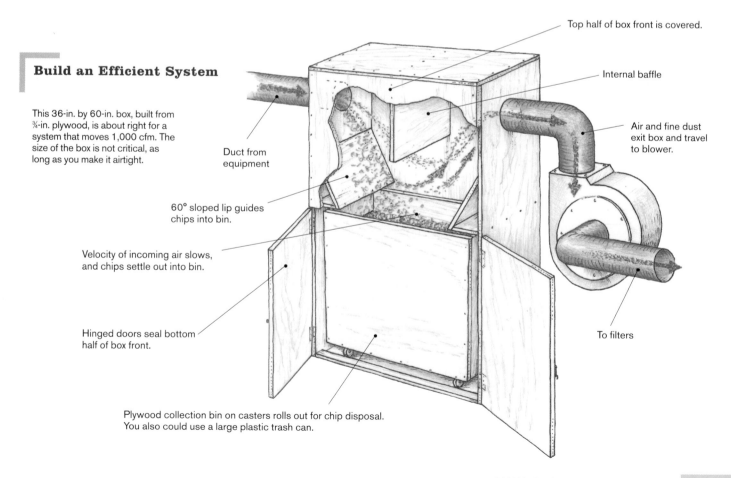

Build an Efficient System

This 36-in. by 60-in. box, built from ¾-in. plywood, is about right for a system that moves 1,000 cfm. The size of the box is not critical, as long as you make it airtight.

Top half of box front is covered.

Internal baffle

Air and fine dust exit box and travel to blower.

Duct from equipment

60° sloped lip guides chips into bin.

Velocity of incoming air slows, and chips settle out into bin.

Hinged doors seal bottom half of box front.

To filters

Plywood collection bin on casters rolls out for chip disposal. You also could use a large plastic trash can.

AIR VOLUME REQUIRED FOR SMALL-SHOP WOODWORKING MACHINES

Machine	Average cfm needed
Tablesaw (8 in. to 12 in.)	350-500
Bandsaw (up to 15 in.)	400
Radial-arm saw (10 in. to 12 in.)	400
Scroll saw	350
Jointer (up to 8 in.)	400
Planer (up to 12 in.)	500
Shaper (½-in. to ¾-in. arbor)	350-450
Lathe	450
Disk (12 in.) or belt sander (6 in.)	400

Note: These numbers are averages based on duct sizes of 4 in. or 5 in. dia. A shaper cutting a crown molding needs more air volume than the same machine trimming a ¼-in. bevel on a shelf edge. Call the manufacturer or an air-handling equipment supplier for exact figures. cfm = cubic feet per minute.

largest dust-producing machine, as shown in the chart on p. 95. Use a 4-in. pipe for most branch ducts; thickness planers need a 5-in. pipe. Connect the branches to a 5-in.- or 6-in.-dia. main duct.

Shop Size Matters If your shop is larger or your collection system is more complicated, the only way to ensure you'll end up with the right size central collector is to design your entire system first. This involves laying out and sizing all the system's main and branch ducts, figuring the cfm needs for all the machines used at one time and calculating the air resistance, or sp losses, in the system.

This process is too complicated to cover in this article, but if you are up to doing the calculations yourself, Air Handling Systems offers a free catalog with instructions for doing the math. The company also sells an inexpensive simple calculator, which works like a slide rule.

If you need more help in designing your system, your local air-handling equipment supplier usually can help. Oneida Air Systems® is one dealer that provides free design services.

Advertised vs. Actual Performance Be aware that the cfm ratings you see in some advertisements reflect the amount of air a collector moves when it's not connected to any ductwork and is operating with no resistance (that's 0 sp). This is known as free-air cfm. Static-pressure ratings also can be misleading because they can represent the pressure loss generated when no air is moving at all, or at 0 cfm.

So how do you really know how much power a collector is capable of generating at a particular cfm? You can ask the manufacturer for a copy of the collector's performance curve. (The performance curve is a graph that plots the actual amount of air the collector will convey under different workloads.) If the dealer can't supply you with one, I suggest buying a unit from one

the collector you'll need. Ribbed, flexible hose generates more friction than straight, smooth-walled duct. Small-diameter ducts add more friction and require more power.

3. How many machines the collection system must handle simultaneously. In most ductwork systems, blast gates control the suction at each workstation. Running several machines at once with two or three gates open, common in a shop with several people, requires more air and power than running a single machine with only one gate open.

If your shop is about the size of a two-car garage and you use only one machine at a time, your central collector should deliver at least 5 in. of sp and about 20% to 50% more cfm than is required by your

who can, or select a model that is sized at least 50% larger than your requirements.

What If Your Collector Isn't Strong Enough?

If you own an underpowered collector, you'll know by the telltale sawdust that accumulates around your equipment. Chips that have settled in the ductwork are another sure sign. If you can't afford to buy a new one, there are a few things that you can do to improve the efficiency of your present collector:

1. Relocate the collector so that it's closer to the machines and floor sweeps. When you reduce the length of ductwork and straighten the number of twists and turns, you lower the resistance to air flow.

2. If dust collection is inadequate at only one machine, such as the planer, move it closer to the blower. Or you could disconnect it from your main system and use a separate dedicated collector to service just that machine.

3. Add more power by connecting two dust collectors in tandem. You'll nearly dou-

The Kind of Fabric Matters

COTTON SATEEN is the least expensive and the least effective at filtering fine dust. It's also more prone to rot and mildew.

WOVEN POLYESTER is more durable but not much better at capturing fine dust.

KNITTED POLYESTER stretches like the material used to make athletic tube socks. It's thick enough for good filtration. The dark lines in this bag are carbon fibers, which help dissipate static electricity.

FELTED POLYESTER has no nap (like wool felt) and tends to be more expensive than woven polyester. Its thickness creates a three-dimensional maze that traps fine dust particles better than all the other samples shown.

ble the force of your system by attaching two units together. Run a hose from the outlet of one blower to the inlet of another. To avoid pressure imbalances, use two identical units.

4. Buy a larger dust bag, or retrofit the fan-inlet plate with a larger duct (both are available from Oneida Air Systems). These methods work especially well with many single-stage collectors. Just like fitting bigger carburetors or mufflers to an auto engine, these new components help the unit convey a larger volume of air. Oneida Air Systems also sells large replacement bags.

Getting Good Filtration

Exhaust from the blower must pass through a filter to remove fine dust and return clean air to the shop. The quality of filtration depends on the kind of fabric material used and the filter's total surface area.

Good and Better Filter Materials If you purchased a single-stage collector a few years ago, it probably came with a cotton sateen or a cotton duck fabric bag. These do a poor job of filtering out dust particles smaller than 30 microns (1 micron is a millionth of a meter).

Dust particles below 10 microns do the most respiratory damage. Most of the collectors sold today come with bags sewn from polyester fabrics—they're better at filtering out harmful dust. Some manufacturers offer them as an alternative to cheaper cotton bags.

Polyester fibers can be woven, knitted or felted (see the photos on p. 94). Filter bags that are made from 12-oz. or 16-oz. felted polyester, singed on the inside by a gas flame to keep the fabric from becoming clogged, are very popular for general woodworking. They can capture 99.5% of very fine dust particles between 0.2 and 2.0 microns. For advice on which fabric is best for your collector, consult with a filter-bag company, such as Midwesco^{SM} Filter Resources.

Dust Cake and Filter Cleaning Fine dust builds up quickly on the inside surface of a filter, forming a film that's known as dust cake. In one way, this is good because the cake acts as a filter in its own right—the buildup of particles blocks the passage of finer and finer dust.

But as a filter becomes more clogged (industry pamphlets call this "blinded"), the air passing through the bag has more difficulty escaping. The mounting static pressure inside the bag actually reduces air flow through the entire collection system. Excess pressure will eventually force fine particles right through the fabric. To keep dust cake from getting too thick, shake the bags occasionally.

Getting Enough Filter Surface Area No amount of cleaning will keep a filter bag working efficiently if there isn't enough surface area. An air-to-cloth ratio is the comparison of a collector's cfm rating to the total square-foot area of its filters.

For general woodworking, an air-to-cloth ratio of 10:1 is about right. So, for every 10 cfm of air delivered, you will need 1 sq. ft. of filter area. Many small-shop dust collectors are skimpy on filter area. It is not uncommon to find single-stage units with air-to-cloth ratios of 35:1 or more. On many models, the lower bag also serves as a dust bin, which further reduces the effective filter area.

How do you address this? In addition to replacing original bags with larger ones, you can gain even more filter-surface area by building a plenum that directs exhaust from the blower to multiple filter bags, or tubes. By using small-diameter tubes, you can add a surprising amount of filter area in a few square feet of shop space. And clean air makes a more enjoyable workplace.

SANDOR NAGYSZALANCZY is a writer and contributing editor to *Fine Woodworking* magazine.

Protecting Your Lungs from Woodworking

My great-grandfather emigrated to this country from the Black Forest of Germany at the end of the 19th century and found work as a finisher for a piano company. That would have been unremarkable except he had only one arm. He was a hard worker and wasn't cut any slack.

The company occasionally held demonstrations that displayed his speed and ability to keep up with other workers. He became so well known for his talent that Mark Twain, who had an eye for unusual characters, hired him to repair some furniture the author had singed with cigars.

In my great-grandfather's day, safety took a back seat to getting the job done. He never wore a dust mask or respirator when he worked. That attitude has prevailed for many generations of woodworkers. I approach woodworking with more caution. For many years, I worked in the pesticide and herbicide industry where a respirator was mandatory. I got used to wearing one,

BY CHARLES W. CALMBACHER

POWER SANDING produces a lot of airborne dust. Seen under 1,200x magnification (inset), wood dust particles are stuck to the strands of a dust mask.

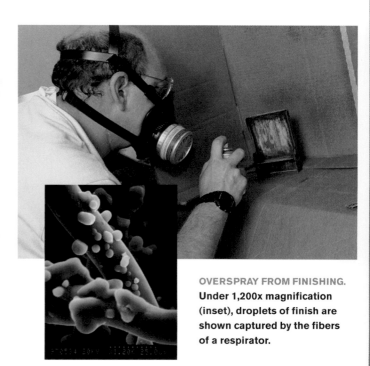

OVERSPRAY FROM FINISHING. Under 1,200x magnification (inset), droplets of finish are shown captured by the fibers of a respirator.

NOT ALL MASKS ARE RATED FOR WOOD DUST. **You might find these low-cost masks near the lumber racks at the home center, but read the label carefully. Some aren't rated for wood dust.**

and I've carried that habit over to my workshop.

Fine Dust Particles Are the Most Dangerous

Wood dust particles created in woodworking come in all sizes, some so small you can't even see them. Sanding machines produce very fine particles; even dull cutting tools will create fine dusts as well as larger chips. Very fine particles cause the most damage to your lungs. Wood dusts are considered a potential carcinogen by the National Institute of Occupational Safety and Health (NIOSH). Some woods, such as Western red cedar, contain resins that are considered toxic. Studies have found that people in the woodworking industry suffer a higher incidence of respiratory system problems, including lung cancer, than the general population.

The nose and bronchial tubes are the body's first line of defense against airborne invaders. There, fine hairlike fibers, called cilia, snag particles. The irritants get trapped in mucus and are expelled through coughing or sneezing. Excessive exposure, however, can irritate the tissues in the nose and bronchial tubes, causing difficulty in breathing and other allergic reactions.

Dusts and mists are most harmful when they enter the lungs, which act like a freeway interchange to other parts of the body, including the bloodstream, kidneys, and central nervous system. Small particles, those ranging in size from 0.5 microns to 5 microns (a sheet of typing paper is about 25 microns thick), are most likely to do this. When dust particles enter the lungs, the body's immune system springs into action and tries to destroy and expel the invaders. Our bodies are quite successful at this. But lung cells can get battle-weary and mutate into cancerous cells when they're overwhelmed by toxins.

NIOSH has revised its standards for respirators because it has been determined that respirator filters are less efficient at filtering dust and mist particles about 0.1 to 0.3 microns in diameter than at filtering smaller or larger particles (see the sidebar on p. 101). New respirators are efficient at capturing all sizes of fine particles. Because you never know exactly what size particles you might face in the workshop if you're running machine tools, it pays to wear some sort of dust mask or respirator. When spray finishing, it's even more important to protect your lungs because you will be faced with fine mist particles as well as potentially hazardous vapors from the chemicals.

Disposable Masks Have Improved

Disposable masks are designed for specific hazards. Some are designed only for pollen and other large particles. It's a safe bet to pick a mask that's been certified by NIOSH. Then you'll know it meets certain standards.

Fitting into a Respirator

Getting a good fit—Masks with two adjustable straps (top and center) usually fit well. A mask that doesn't seal flat against the face (bottom) will allow dust or mist to escape past the filter.

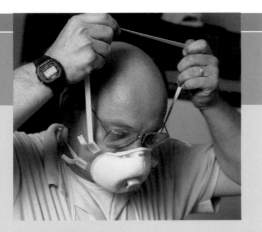

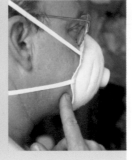

Three Kinds of Respirators

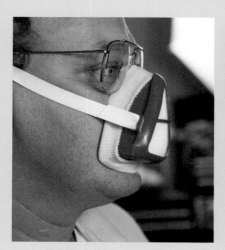

QUARTER-FACE MASK. This mask seals well because of its soft body and fabric covering. The filter is replaceable.

HALF-FACE MASK. These respirators are usually made of soft rubber or silicone and have replaceable filter cartridges.

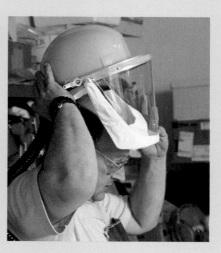

FULL-FACE PROTECTION. Powered air-purifying respirators deliver a constant supply of filtered air.

Though often referred to as paper dust masks, these disposables are made of a variety of materials including finely woven paper, plastics, and polymers. These filters come in many styles: from the basic mask with an elastic headband to more elaborate, molded units with exhalation valves, silicon seals, and adjustable headbands. Prices for these respirators range from about 15 cents to several dollars each. The most inexpensive masks, made of thin materials and a flimsy bendable metal strap over the nose bridge, often don't seal well. Fiber masks, made of thicker materials molded to conform to the shape of the face, provide a better fit and improved seal. Some come with one-way valves, which make breathing easier and help prevent fogging of glasses. Masks equipped with two adjustable straps offer a more secure fit than those with a single elastic band. People who have beards,

however, won't get a good seal with any of these masks.

Replace a disposable mask when breathing through it becomes difficult. Don't try to extend the life of a mask by vacuuming or washing it. Doing so will only break down the material and make the mask ineffective.

Air-Purifying Cartridge Respirators

Air-purifying cartridge respirators come in three basic styles: quarter-, half-, and full-face designs. These make you look like a serious toxic avenger. The quarter- and half-face models cover the nose and mouth; the full-face models offer eye protection as well. Again, many of these will not seal well if the wearer has a beard. To be effective, respirators must seal against bare skin.

The quarter-face air-purifying respirator is usually made of rubber, silicones or plastic (see the above left photo). It is designed to

fit over the nose and mouth, and it rests on the chin. It comes with a replaceable filter that will block out dusts and nontoxic mists. These respirators cost about $5 and replacement filters are usually available for about $1 or less.

The half-face respirator covers the nose and mouth and fits under the chin. Outfitted with the appropriate cartridges, it can protect against very fine particles, toxic vapors, mists, and some gasses (see the center photo on p. 99). A respirator body with a pair of filters costs $25 to $40. Cartridges cost $8 to $20 per pair.

These are a good choice for woodworking because they have soft rubber or silicone seals and adjustable straps. A good fit is important with a respirator, and except for those with beards, half-face respirators will fit almost anyone.

Although half-face respirators serve most woodworkers well, there is a mask that provides even more protection: the full-face respirator, available from industrial equipment suppliers. It seals along the forehead, temples, cheeks, and under the chin. A full-face respirator has the additional advantage of built-in eye and face protection. The body of these devices costs from $150 to $250. Cartridges are $8 to $20 per pair.

Powered Air-Purifying Respirators Are Comfortable

Powered air-purifying respirators (PAPRs) come in several styles: half-face, full-face, with a hood or with a face-shield and a seal around the face. These respirators (see the photos on p. 99) have battery-powered fans that draw air through replaceable filters. Depending on the model, they can filter dusts, mists, and other hazards. (NIOSH is still developing new standards for these.) Like full-face respirators, these offer excellent protection. If you wear glasses or have a beard, a full-face, hooded PAPR may give you the best fit and, therefore, the best protection. I prefer PAPRs for woodworking

because they reduce the strain of breathing through a filter.

PAPRs are available through professional tool stores, woodworking equipment suppliers, safety equipment companies, and directly from some manufacturers. The cost of these respirators varies based on the design—the more hazards they guard against, the higher the cost. Prices range from approximately $150 to $500. Cartridges range in price from $8 to more than $20.

PAPRs pump filtered fresh air toward your face, which makes them comfortable to wear, even in warm weather. But pay attention to the sound of the fan; if it sounds like it's beginning to strain, it probably means that it's time to change the filter.

Filters Are Made for a Variety of Applications

It's important to pick the right filter for the job. When spraying lacquer, for example, be sure to get cartridges rated for organic vapors. Those come with charcoal filters that capture toxic vapors, which even the best dust mask. You shouldn't be able to detect the smell of a finishing product when breathing through a respirator fitted with the proper cartridges. If you can, it's time to replace the cartridges. They cannot be cleaned.

There's not a cartridge available for every chemical you might use in the workshop. If you're working with methanol or products containing isocyanates, such as urethanes and polyurethanes, have plenty of fresh air circulation—there isn't a NIOSH-approved filter cartridge to trap those vapors. A respirator, however, will help somewhat by capturing mists from overspray.

It's possible to fill an enclosed room, such as a spray booth, with a high concentration of mists and vapors, which will overwhelm an air-purifying respirator. Air-purifying respirators do not supply oxygen, they only filter contaminants. If you suspect you are creating high concentrations of chemical contaminants, you should have a professional test for oxygen levels.

Because NIOSH has issued new standards for respirators, and old and new models are still on the market, it's confusing sorting through all the numbers and alphabet soup printed on the labels.

On old-style disposable respirators rated for dusts and mists, the label or packaging will have the code TC-21C, followed by some numbers. The 21C tells you it's an old-style mask, and possibly less effective than the newer models. New masks are coded differently, and even the most basic NIOSH-approved dust mask will capture 95% of the particles at 0.3 microns, the most penetrating size.

If you have a cartridge-style mask, there are many specialty filters available. For capturing fine dusts, high-efficiency particulate air (HEPA®) filters are a good choice. Most of the HEPA filters manufactured under the old standards will meet the highest level of the new guidelines, which require filters to capture 99.97% of dusts in the 0.3 micron size.

* Note: price estimates are from 1997.

CHARLES W. CALMBACHER is an environmental, health, and safety consultant and teaches at the University of Georgia at Athens. He lives in Lawrenceville, Georgia.

USE THE PROPER CARTRIDGE FOR THE CHEMICAL HAZARD. For spraying lacquer, organic vapor cartridges, which contain carbon filters, will trap hazardous fumes.

New Standards for Respirators

The National Institute for Occupational Safety and Health (NIOSH) issued new standards for respirators that went into effect July 10, 1995, and allowed a 3-year grandfather period. Dust masks and cartridges for respirators manufactured after July 10, 1998, must meet the new standards. Consumers will continue to see older products sold after that date because retailers will be allowed to deplete their stocks. Respirators that meet the new guidelines are already on the market.

The new regulations require approved filters to be at least 95% efficient at capturing particles 0.3 microns in size, the most penetrating. Disposable masks that meet the new standards are rated with a letter designation followed by a number, such as N95. Masks beginning with an N are for use where there is no oil present in the air, masks labeled with an R are resistant to oil mists, and P is for masks that are even more resistant to oils. The numbers refer to the efficiency of the respirators: 95%, 99%, and 100% (actually 99.97%) efficient. Cartridge-style filters must meet the same standards. Because cartridges are available for a host of hazards, they are labeled with additional information.

Manufacturers are making new cartridges to fit all or most masks on the market. The new standards apply to all particulate filters for non–powered air-purifying respirators. NIOSH may work on new standards for powered respirators in the future.

DUST MASK THAT COMPLIES WITH NEW STANDARDS. This NIOSH-approved dust mask is rated N95. That means it's not oil resistant, and it's 95% efficient at capturing dust particles as small as 0.3 microns.

Dust Collection for the One-Man Shop

BY ANATOLE BURKIN

Don't throw away the broom just yet. Even the best dust-collection system won't eliminate the need for occasional sweeping. A good system, however, will keep the broom and your lungs from wearing out prematurely.

There are two main points to consider when choosing a dust collector. First, figure out the air-volume requirements of the machines in your shop (see the chart on p. 107). Next, decide on what kind of hookups you are going to use: flexible hose, PVC pipe, or metal duct.

To see what size and type of collector would best suit a one-man shop, I gathered a sampling of machines, from 1-hp single-stage units to 2-hp two-stage collectors, including one cyclone: Delta (1½ hp single stage), Dust Boy (2 hp two stage), Jet Equipment & Tools® (2 hp single stage), Oneida (1½ hp cyclone), and SECO™ UFO-90 (1 hp single stage). I used the collectors with my tools, which include a 10-in. cabinet saw, a 15-in. planer, an 8-in. jointer, and a 16-in. bandsaw.

The horsepower rating is a fairly reliable guide to the performance of a dust collector (see the chart on p. 163). Hookups, however, are everything. Too much flexible hose will rob even a big collector of power. PVC pipes, in short runs, work fine with a sufficiently powered collector, 1½ hp or more. Metal duct, not unexpectedly, performs best. Even an 8-year-old, 1-hp collector can collect chips from machines 25 ft. away when hooked up to a properly designed system. Using a 1-hp collector this way may seem misguided, like putting a racing exhaust system on a subcompact car, but the experiment illustrates how you don't have to spend a fortune to get decent results. Every shop is different, of course, and your results may vary, so use my findings as guidelines, not absolutes.

1-hp Single-Stage Collectors

The biggest sawdust producer in my shop is a 15-in. planer. And even a 1-hp single-stage dust collector can handle that machine, hooked up with about 6 ft. of 4-in.-dia. flexible hose. I borrowed a new UFO-90, same as my old collector, to see if anything had been changed. It's still the same machine, rated at 650 cubic feet per minute (cfm) by the manufacturer, but when hooked up to 6 ft. of flexible hose, it moves about 420 cfm. That's slightly less than the 500 cfm recommended for a 15-in. planer, but 90% of the time the 1-hp collector can handle it because I rarely plane 15-in.-wide stock.

One-hp single-stage collectors cost about $200. Some woodworkers buy two

1-HP COLLECTORS. Small, portable collectors are easy to move around the shop. Make connections to one tool at a time using a short piece of flexible hose.

units and station them strategically in their shop. At 82 decibels (measured at 8 ft.), a 1-hp dust collector isn't much noisier than a vacuum cleaner, and each one takes up about 3 sq. ft. of shop space.

I also used the 1-hp collector with a PVC duct system (4-in.-dia. pipe and fittings) and measured the moving air volume at the tablesaw-jointer connection, which is at the end of about 25 ft. of pipe and hose. At that distance, because of increased resistance, the air volume drops to under 300 cfm, less than recommended for

Three Styles of Dust Collectors

The most economical and biggest-selling dust collectors are the two-bag, single-stage models. Single stage means the dust is sucked through the impeller (fan) and dumped into the lower bag. The upper bag collects fine sawdust and lets the exhaust air back into the shop.

Two-stage collectors are the next step up. The motor and impeller sit atop a barrel. Chips enter the barrel and are directed downward, although the swirling air inside may occasionally move smaller chips upward. A filter bag hangs off to one side and collects the finest dust.

Two-stage cyclones are at the top of the evolutionary chain. The motor and impeller sit atop a cone-shaped canister, the cyclone, which is connected to a trash can below. Chips or other large debris enter the cyclone and swirl downward, avoiding the impeller. The longer the cyclonic chamber, the greater its effectiveness at slowing down and separating large particles. Air is filtered either by a pleated internal cartridge or by one or more felt bags hanging off to the side of the machine. Internal-cartridge cyclones use the least amount of floor space. The upper bags or cartridge filters of all collectors must be shaken out occasionally to remove fine dust.

DANGERS OF SINGLE-STAGE COLLECTORS

Debris entering a single-stage collector passes through the impeller, many of which are made of steel. Even a small bit of metal, such as a screw, can cause a spark when it hits a steel impeller. Dust-collector explosions are rare, but the potential is there. Debris, metal or otherwise, not only makes a racket when it hits an impeller but also imparts stress on the bearing and will shorten its life. I heard of a woodworker whose collector's sheet-metal housing was punctured by a screw that entered the impeller.

One way to reduce the risk of fire is to choose a single-stage collector with a plastic or aluminum impeller. Although the impeller itself won't cause a spark, metal debris striking the steel housing may have the same effect. Steel impellers are fine, however, if you avoid using the dust collector to sweep up miscellaneous debris off the floor or workbench.

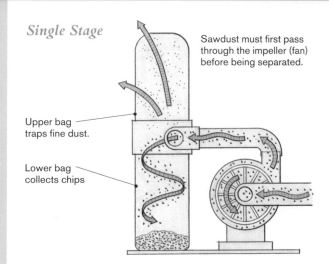

Single Stage

Sawdust must first pass through the impeller (fan) before being separated.

Upper bag traps fine dust.

Lower bag collects chips

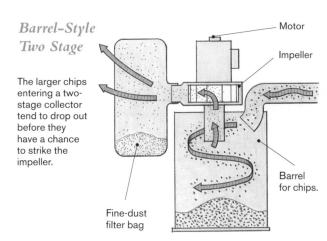

Barrel-Style Two Stage

Motor

Impeller

The larger chips entering a two-stage collector tend to drop out before they have a chance to strike the impeller.

Fine-dust filter bag

Barrel for chips.

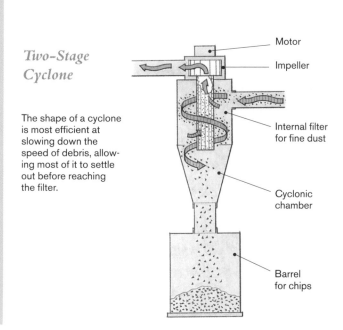

Two-Stage Cyclone

Motor

Impeller

The shape of a cyclone is most efficient at slowing down the speed of debris, allowing most of it to settle out before reaching the filter.

Internal filter for fine dust

Cyclonic chamber

Barrel for chips

woodworking tools. In reality, however, one can live with that. But if I'm face-jointing wide boards, the collector can't always handle the volume, and chips jam the jointer's dust port. Maybe 80% of the time it works okay.

When I hooked up the 1-hp collector to a newly installed metal duct system, with my tools in the same configuration as before, I was really surprised. The air volume was back up to 360 cfm, very acceptable. Then I hooked up my old 1-hp collector, which is outfitted with oversized felt bags (available from Oneida Air Systems) that improve airflow and capture fine dust (see the sidebar below), and I measured almost 400 cfm. That's a significant gain.

Hook Up 1½-hp Collectors to Runs of Hose or Duct

As you might imagine, hooked up to one machine at a time, a 1½-hp collector does not have any trouble removing chips, even with a long (12-ft.) run of hose. Delta rates its 1½-hp collector at 1,200 cfm, a number that is derived in a lab, not under real shop conditions (for more on manufacturer specs, see sidebar on p. 106). Hooked up to a 6-ft. run of 4-in.-dia. flexible hose, I measured about 500 cfm with the Delta and 470 cfm using an Oneida Air Systems 1½-hp cyclone collector. Cyclones and two-stage collectors have slightly more internal air resistance; hence the lower cfm reading. That's about what you can expect from any 1½-hp collector hooked up to 4-in.-dia. hose.

I also hooked up the 1½-hp collectors to two machines running simultaneously. Performance ranged from good to so-so, depending on how much sawdust was being spit out by my tools. The best way to direct maximum airflow to the tool being used is to attach a blast gate to each hose.

Hooked up to a PVC duct system (a run of about 25 ft. of pipe), both the Delta

1 1/2-HP COLLECTORS. **Although collectors in this power category may occasionally be used with two tools simultaneously, for best performance, use blast gates and run one tool at a time.**

Go with Felt Bags

The standard bags issued with most dust collectors are good for capturing particles of 25 to 30 microns or bigger. A micron is 1/1,000,000th of a meter in length; looked at another way, the paper this article is printed on is about 25 microns thick. Fine dust blows right through filter fabric, back into the shop. Dust particles under 10 microns in size are the most harmful because they can get past the respiratory tract and enter your lungs. Unless you wear a dust mask while woodworking, toss out the stock bags and replace them with felt bags rated at 5 microns or less.

FABRIC VS. FELT. A fabric bag, left, has less thickness and is more porous. Felt, right, does a much better job of filtering out very fine dust.

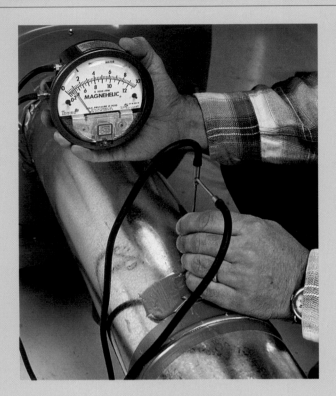

MEASUREMENTS WERE TAKEN WITH A DIAL-GAUGE MANOMETER (A PRESSURE GAUGE) AND PITOT TUBE. The chart below compares the performance of a few dust collectors when using hose, PVC pipe and metal duct.

MAKING SENSE OF MANUFACTURER SPECS

There's a fair amount of misleading marketing specs on dust collectors. When an ad says a collector is rated at 1,200 cfm, what does it mean? Not much, really. Cfm stands for cubic feet per minute, a measure of the volume of air moving past a point of reference. The cfm figure needs to be put in the context of the amount of resistance, or friction, present (called static pressure, or SP). Air moving through duct or hose encounters resistance, just as a person would slipping down a water slide. The more bends and bumps, the slower the ride or the lower the air velocity and volume. Many manufacturers rate their machines without bags or duct attached.

While trying out a number of dust collectors, I measured their performances under real working conditions, using flexible hose, PVC pipe or metal duct in my 420-sq.-ft. shop (see the chart below). The resistance readings ranged from 3 in. to 5 in. I also measured collectors hooked up to a straight piece of 6-in.-dia. metal duct, just to get a baseline, highest-possible performance figure.

Collectors ranging in size from 1 hp to 2 hp have impellers (fans) sized from 10 in. dia. to 12 in. dia. All

PERFORMANCE OF DUST COLLECTORS UNDER VARYING CONDITIONS

Horsepower	6 ft. from collector, 6-in.-dia. straight metal duct*	6 ft. from collector, 4-in.-dia. flexible hose	6 ft. from collector, two runs of 4-in.-dia. flexible hose	25 ft. from collector, at jointer hookup, 4-in.-dia. PVC pipe	25 ft. from collector, at jointer hookup, 5-in.-dia. metal duct
1 hp single stage	550 cfm	Excellent	Fair	Fair	Excellent
1½ hp single stage	825 cfm	Excellent	Good	Good	Excellent
1½ hp cyclone	700 cfm	Excellent	Good	Good	Excellent
2 hp single stage	980 cfm	Excellent	Excellent	Excellent	Excellent
2 hp two stage	825 cfm	Excellent	Good	Good	Excellent

Fair: under 300 cfm   Good: 325 cfm to 350 cfm   Excellent: more than 350 cfm
* Bags or filters attached with a light coating of sawdust present.

things being equal (motor speed and impeller design), a bigger impeller coupled with a bigger motor will move more air than a smaller pairing. There are some differences among collectors; to learn more, ask a manufacturer for an impeller performance chart.

As soon as any collector is hooked up in the shop, performance declines in relation to the length and type of hookup. That's why smooth-walled metal duct, with wide-radius elbows and wyes, is better than PVC pipe.

AIR-VOLUME REQUIREMENTS OF MACHINES

Tool	cfm needed
10-in. tablesaw	350
6-in. or 8-in. jointer	300-450
12-in. planer	350
15-in. planer	500
Drill press	350
14-in. or 16-in. bandsaw	350
Radial-arm saw	350-500
12-in. disc sander	350
12-in. to 24-in. drum sander	300-500
Oscillating spindle sander	350
Floor sweep	350

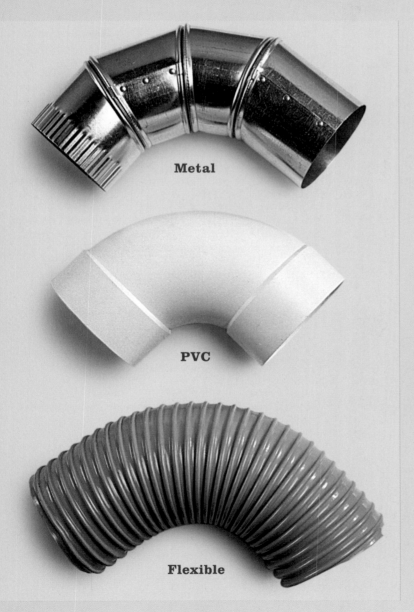

Metal

PVC

Flexible

MATERIALS THAT AFFECT AIRFLOW. The metal elbow (top), which is designed for central dust-collection systems, has a gentle sweep, which lowers resistance to airflow. Plastic PVC pipe (center) has a tighter-radius bend and restricts airflow more. Ribbed flexible pipe (bottom) also disturbs airflow, up to three times as much as metal.

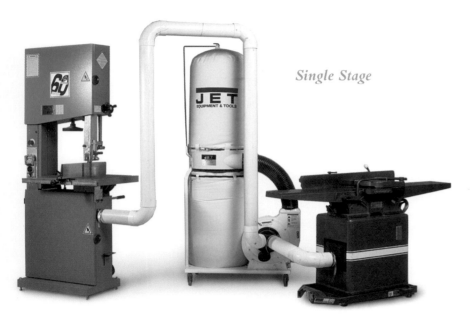

Single Stage

2-HP COLLECTORS. Many 2-hp collectors can handle two tools at once. Although 4-in.-dia. PVC pipe is not the best duct material, satisfactory results can be obtained when connected to a 2-hp collector.

Barrel-Style Two Stage

and Oneida collectors captured most of the sawdust when running one tool.

A 1½-hp Delta collector costs about $350. A two-stage unit such as the Oneida costs almost twice as much. Penn State Industries also sells a cyclone collector. (For more on the advantages of two-stage collectors vs. single-stage units, see the sidebar on p. 104.)

Both 1½-hp collectors performed exceptionally well when connected to metal duct and used with one tool at a time. With two blast gates open, the air volume

dropped and was insufficient to operate two big machines at once.

The larger-volume bags or canisters of 1½-hp collectors hold a lot of material, about 30 gal. worth, which means fewer trips to the compost pile, a big advantage over the 1-hp machines that hold about half of that. A 1½-hp single-stage collector takes up about 7 sq. ft. of shop space. But a vertically stacked two-stage cyclone such as the Oneida takes up only 3½ sq. ft. of shop space, a big plus in a small shop. More horsepower does mean more noise; both registered 85 decibels at 8 ft. The Delta comes wired for 115 volts but can be switched over to 230 volts. The Oneida comes without cable or switch. It can be wired to run on either current.

A 2-hp Unit Can Sometimes Handle Two Machines at Once

Hooked up to two 6-ft. runs of 4-in.-dia. hoses, a 2-hp single-stage collector draws over 350 cfm from each port, plenty for many woodworking machines. The 2-hp two-stage Dust Boy didn't match the power of the 2-hp single-stage Jet machine, although it has other qualities that may be preferable (see the sidebar on p. 104). When I connected the 2-hp units to the PVC duct system, they, too, were robbed of considerable power, but one machine could be operated at a time with satisfactory results.

When connected to a metal duct system, the Jet collector moved a lot of air, 570 cfm at the tablesaw-jointer connection (after about 25 ft. of duct). With two blast gates open, the air volume was reduced to less than 300 cfm, still acceptable for some operations. The Dust Boy produced slightly lower readings but still had more than enough power to run one tool at a time in any configuration. If you regularly operate more than one machine simultaneously, it would be wise to look at 3-hp or bigger dust collectors.

The 2-hp machines are no noisier than the 1½-hp collectors. They cost more, however. The Jet is priced at $400; the Dust Boy sells for about $650. Most 2-hp collectors come wired for 230 volts. The Dust Boy can be run at either 115 volts or 230 volts.

Choosing Among the Options

On the matter of choosing a dust collector, a two-stage cyclone gets my top vote. A small cyclone collector takes up less room, is easy to empty, and runs clean. For example, on all of the single-stage units, even after running them for only an hour, fine dust appeared on the machine and in the area around it. That's because it's difficult to get a perfect seal between the bag and housing. The Oneida cyclone, outfitted with an internal filter, rubber gaskets, and wide metal ring clamps, seals better.

Two-stage units such as the Dust Boy (Delta also makes a two-stage collector) are also nice and compact. The Dust Boy takes up 6 sq. ft. and less vertical space than most collectors. The Dust Boy (as does the Oneida) comes with a Leeson® motor and cast-aluminum housing and impeller (fan), and the sturdy plastic barrel holds a lot of debris, 55 gal. worth. Before it can be emptied, however, the heavy motor and housing must be lifted off.

Removing the lower bag of a single-stage collector is an easy matter of loosening a band clamp. The real fun begins when you try to reattach it. If you've ever had to put your pants on with an arm in a cast, you'll get the idea. The lower bag must be wrapped around the metal waist of the machine and held in place before the clamp can be cinched. Some manufacturers, such

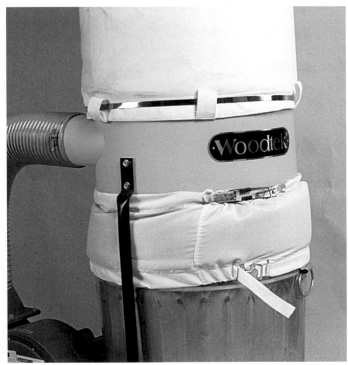

BETTER CONNECTIONS. The Oneida cyclone collector's trash barrel is connected by a large metal ring, which simplifies reattachment (left). Woodworker's Supply[SM] sells a clamp-on skirt accessory that is used with a 30-gal. trash can (above). The skirt is easier to reattach than a standard lower bag.

Designing a Central Dust-Collection System

Oneida Air Systems designed my ductwork, which is typical for a one-room shop under 500 sq. ft. The ductwork begins with a 6-in.-dia. pipe connected to the collector. At the first wye (split), the duct reduces to 5-in.-dia. branches. The 5-in.-dia. pipes serve the biggest tools (jointer, tablesaw, and planer), even though they all have 4-in.-dia. dust ports, which ensure good air volume to the machines. Also, you can change the dust port to a 5-in.-dia. connection for better performance. A 5-in.-dia. to 4-in.-dia. reducer is used to make the transition.

The 4-in.-dia. branches that split off the 5-in.-dia. line serve smaller tools, such as the bandsaw and router table. Blast gates are installed at each tool. The final connections were made with flexible hose, which allows me to move my tools around.

I used 24-gauge (mostly) snap-lock pipe, spot-welded fittings, and aluminum blast gates, which are available from many companies. (Avoid lighter-gauge metal duct designed for heating or cooling systems; it can collapse under vacuum.)

A higher-quality system will employ 22-gauge spiral pipe and welded fittings, which are stiffer and more airtight, and yes, they cost more. Quick-Fit™ duct supplies from Nordfab are also premium priced, but the components go together easily and don't require duct tape or caulk.

Although individual 24-gauge components aren't that expensive (a 5-ft. run of 5-in.-dia. snap-lock pipe costs about $8), it all adds up. A basic three-machine setup may be had for a few hundred dollars. A system for half a dozen tools and a floor sweep may cost $500 or more.

To help illustrate the photos in this article, an orange/black flex hose was used to make connections from pipe to tools; black flex hose, however, works fine. It's best to use a minimum of hose because it produces about three times the friction of metal pipe. Friction will reduce the performance of the system. All pipe seams and connections must be sealed with caulk or duct tape. Clear silicone caulk is a good choice because it's virtually invisible and is easy to remove.

Design Help Is Available

Designing the ductwork for a central dust-collection system can involve a lot of calculations. For those of us who skipped math class, there's help available.

- Air Handling Systems of Woodbridge, Conn., has an online duct calculator program (www.airhand.com). The company outlines the concepts of duct design in a four-page brochure.

- Oneida Air Systems of Syracuse, N.Y., will design a duct system free of charge for its customers (www.oneida-air.com). All that's required is a shop drawing showing the types and locations of woodworking machines.

- Nordfab of Thomasville, N.C., manufacturers of the Quick-Fit line of duct and fittings, offers a free design service. The company has a downloadable program (www.nordfab.com), but you need a CAD program to run it. The company also offers a peel-and-stick shop layout kit for analog woodworkers.

- If you wish to tackle duct design yourself, all of the necessary information can be found in *Woodshop Dust Control* by Sandor Nagyszalanczy (The Taunton Press, 1996).

NO SCREWS OR RIVETS NEEDED. Quick-Fit duct pipe from Nordfab is assembled using gasketed clamps.

as Jet, add an elastic band inside the lower bag to facilitate reattachment somewhat.

Woodworker's Supply tried to solve the lower-bag problem with a clamp-on skirt accessory. The skirt and a standard 30-gal. trash can replace the lower bag. Because the skirt remains attached to the collector's housing, it's easy to cinch the lower belt that attaches the skirt to the trash can. I just wish the skirt were made of felt rather than the more porous woven fabric. This setup will reduce the air volume (the collector "breathes" through both bags) when using the stock upper bag. With a larger upper bag, I found that the cfm readings were not compromised. But if you happen to vacuum up any offcuts, they will make quite a racket rattling around in a metal trash can.

Although many woodworkers, myself included, have used PVC drainpipe for duct without mishap, experts warn against using the material. The connectors (elbows and wyes) restrict airflow, and the material builds up a static charge, which may cause a spark and set off an explosion. (Running grounded copper wire inside the pipe reduces the hazard.) Use PVC at your own risk. Metal duct and fittings are obviously better and will also last longer. I've broken half a dozen plastic blast gates in as many years. If you're on a tight budget, go with flexible hose or build a metal duct system in stages, starting with only a couple of hookups. Your collector will work more efficiently, and so will you.

ANATOLE BURKIN is a senior editor of *Fine Woodworking* magazine.

Sources

Air Handling Systems
800-367-3828
www.airhand.com
Duct supplies and duct design

American Fabric Filter Co.
800-367-3591
www.americanfabricfilter.com
Custom-made dust bags

Delta
800-438-2486
www.deltawoodworking.com
Dust collectors

Dust Boy
800-232-3878
www.dustboy.com
Dust collectors

Highland Hardware
800-241-6748
www.tools-for-woodworking.com
Dust collectors

Jet Equipment & Tools
800-274-6848
www.jetequipment.com
Dust collectors and supplies

Kraemer Tools
800-443-6443
www.kraemertool.com
Dust collectors and supplies
(Canada)

Leneave Machinery
800-442-2302
Dust collectors

Nordfab
800-532-0830
www.ductingsystems.com
Quick-Fit duct supplies

Oneida Air Systems
800-732-4065
www.oneida-air.com
Dust collectors, duct supplies and duct design

Penn State Industries
800-377-7297
www.pennstateind.com
Dust collectors and supplies

Powermatic®
800-248-0144
www.powermatic.com
Dust collectors

Sunhill Machinery
800-929-4321
www.sunhillmachinery.com
Dust collectors and supplies

Wilke Machinery
800-235-2100
www.wilkemach.com
Dust collectors and supplies

Woodworker's Supply
800-645-9292
www.woodworker.com
Dust collectors and supplies

Dust Detector

BY ROBERT S. WRIGHT

After we moved into our new house, my wife decided that we needed a change in bedroom furniture. As I contemplated the months—years?—it would take me to complete this challenge, my pride was dealt a sudden blow. My wife said she wanted to buy a

bedroom set made in the Queen Anne style. Well, I had to admit that carving shells was not part of my repertoire (yet), so I gave in. Meanwhile, as a sop to my ego, I got the go-ahead to enhance my shop with a bandsaw, new saw fence, and, most important, a dust collector to keep

Shopmade Automatic Switch

Turn off all power before working inside the service panel. If this is unfamiliar territory, call an electrician. This diagram shows the wiring for a 240-volt woodworking machine and a 240-volt dust collector. For a 120-volt tool, substitute the second power wire with a neutral wire (see the drawing on p. 116)

240-volt outlet for tool

Override switch for dust collector

Service panel

Double-pole circuit breaker (240 volts) for tool

Double-pole circuit breaker (240 volts) for dust collector

Hot wires

Neutral wires

Ground wire

240-volt outlet for dust collector

Incoming power

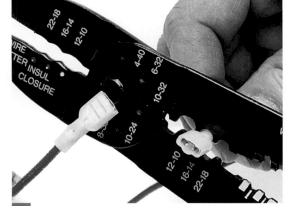

SENSOR AND RELAY HAVE 1/4-IN. SPADE LUGS.
Female connectors are attached to the wire with a crimping tool.

1. Connect Tools to the Current Sensor

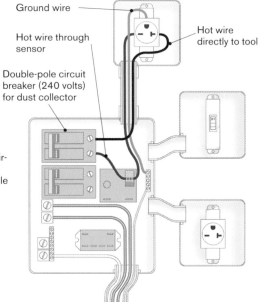

Ground wire

Hot wire through sensor

Hot wire directly to tool

Double-pole circuit breaker (240 volts) for dust collector

One hot wire from each tool circuit is routed through the sensor's loop. The loop can handle about six 12-gauge wires.

2. Wire the Relay for the Dust Collector

The dust collector must have its own circuit breaker.

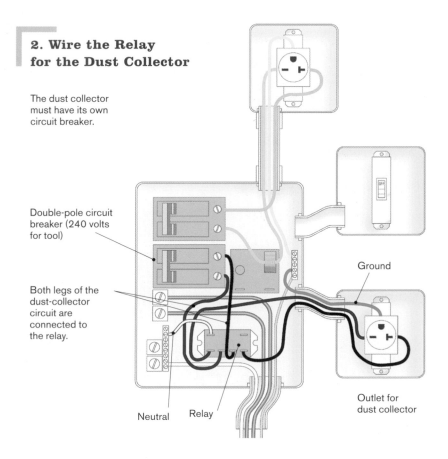

Double-pole circuit breaker (240 volts for tool)

Both legs of the dust-collector circuit are connected to the relay.

Ground

Neutral

Relay

Outlet for dust collector

3. Connect the Relay to the Sensor

Choose a relay that's rated for 240 volts.

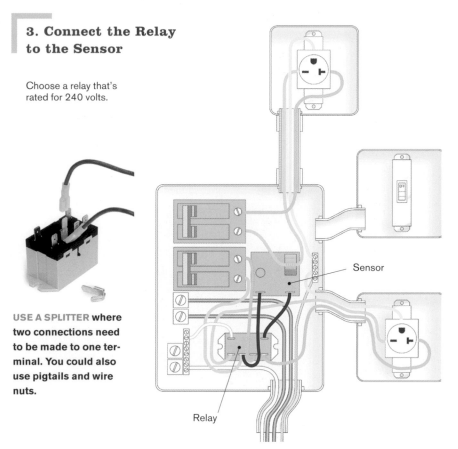

USE A SPLITTER where two connections need to be made to one terminal. You could also use pigtails and wire nuts.

Sensor

Relay

the new home clean. I love that new bedroom set!

The new tools worked out fine, except for one thing: Even though I placed the switch for the dust collector in a central location, I often neglected to turn it on. I needed a better solution. The Internet can be a good place to find answers to technical problems, and this dilemma proved to be no exception. After some searching, I discovered I could buy an off-the-shelf current sensor that would serve as the heart of a shopmade automatic switch for my dust collector. The rest of the parts include a relay, a basic on/off switch, single electrical box, and some wire. The total cost: a little more than $50.

The concept is simple and works like similar products on the market, which cost four times as much. A current sensor is placed inside the service panel (or in a separate panel next to it) that serves the shop. One hot wire from each tool that is connected to a dust collector runs through the sensor. When a tool is fired up, the sensor detects the current running through the hot wire. A signal is sent to the relay, which turns on the dust collector. It's that easy. Blast gates are your responsibility.

It's important to choose the correct relay based on the horsepower and voltage of your dust collector. And because the sensor works by reading current, you'll need to isolate each tool on its own circuit. For home shops that share electrical circuits with home appliances, my system may be more work or expense than you're willing to absorb. An aftermarket radio-controlled on/off switch might be a better choice.

A few words of caution: If you don't know anything about electrical equipment, get some help. There is a danger of electrical shock and all the mishaps associated with it, including death. Some locales do not allow you to do your own electrical work; you're required to hire a licensed contractor to do it. When in doubt, contact your local authorities. Be sure to turn off the power before working around any live connections. Once I gathered up all the parts, the job took me about an hour.

Install the Sensor in a Service Panel

After turning off the power, remove the cover of the service panel. Be sure to place the screws in a safe place. It is amazing how far they can travel without legs.

Locate and mark the wires that power woodworking machines with dust collection. If there are tools on a trigger circuit that should not set off the dust collector, put them on new or different circuits. (Because the current sensor can be adjusted for sensitivity from 2 amps to 20 amps, it is possible to run other tools without setting off the sensor as long as the unwanted tools are of a lower amperage rating.)

Find an area near the wires to install the current sensor module. Attach it with a pan-head sheet-metal screw. Position the relay to allow easy routing of wires.

Detach one hot wire for each circuit (use only one hot wire from 240-volt tools) from its circuit breaker. Route the wire through the sensor's loop, then reconnect it to its circuit breaker. The current sensor has a loop big enough for about six 12-gauge THHN wires.

Next, install the relay. If there's no room in the service panel, place the relay in a smaller electrical box and connect it to the main box with a piece of conduit.

Install the override switch in a logical place in the shop. Run conduit and two 12-gauge wires from the switch to the service panel. The switch allows the collector to be turned on for other uses, such as with a floor sweep, or to be used with tools not connected to the sensor.

If the dust collector's circuit breaker is far from the shop area, and the dust collec-

4. Install an Override Switch

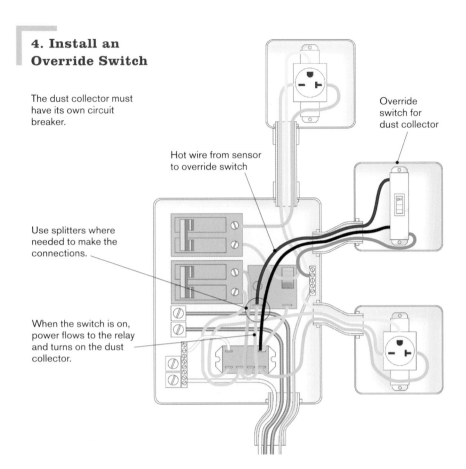

The dust collector must have its own circuit breaker.

Hot wire from sensor to override switch

Override switch for dust collector

Use splitters where needed to make the connections.

When the switch is on, power flows to the relay and turns on the dust collector.

tor does not have its own on/off switch or a plug, install a disconnect switch in the power line close to the dust collector as a safety measure.

The wiring for the relay is slightly different for a 120-volt collector than it is for a 240-volt collector (see the drawing on p. 116). Use crimp-on spade lug connectors to connect to the sensor module and relay. Be sure to orient the override switch in a way that won't confuse. Normally, the up position means "on." The wires used to connect all of the parts have to be large enough for the circuit breaker that powers everything. Twelve-gauge wire is the minimum size required for a 20-amp circuit.

Time for the acid test. Set the sensor's sensitivity knob to 2 amps. Reinstall the cover on the service panel. Verify that the override switch is in its off position.

Wiring for 120-Volt System

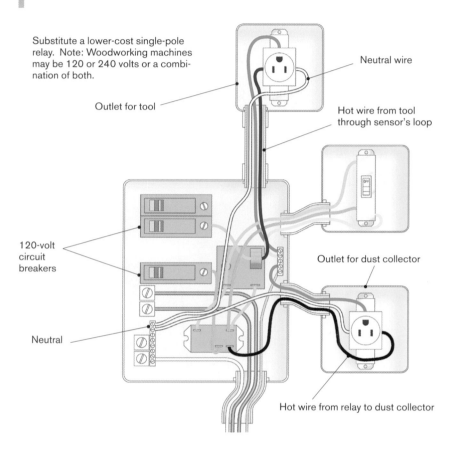

Substitute a lower-cost single-pole relay. Note: Woodworking machines may be 120 or 240 volts or a combination of both.

Outlet for tool

Neutral wire

Hot wire from tool through sensor's loop

120-volt circuit breakers

Neutral

Outlet for dust collector

Hot wire from relay to dust collector

Restore power to the panel, then turn on all of the circuit breakers. The dust collector should not start. If it does, be sure that the override switch is installed correctly. Test the current-sensor circuit by starting the tools connected to the dust collector. The collector should turn on and off with each tool. Test the override switch. If everything works as planned, power up some smaller tools that share circuits with dust-collected tools. If they set off the collector, fiddle with the sensitivity knob of the sensor and see if you can dial them out selectively. It's a trial-and-error process and will be more successful with smaller, portable tools.

ROBERT S. WRIGHT enjoys recreational woodworking at his home in San Marcos, California.

Parts List for Automatic Switch

Part	Cost
SSAC current sensor TCSHAA	$38
Power relay; Grainger part no. 3A355	$11
Common household switch	$1
Single-gang electrical box	$1.50
Female ¼-in. spade lugs	$2
Wire nuts or splitters	$1
If needed: 12-gauge THHN wire, conduit	

* Note that price estimates are from 2000

- The current sensor and power relays are available from many electronics distributors. Grainger (800-225-5994) is listed for convenience. Contact SSAC via its Web site (www.ssac.com) or call (315-638-1300).

- Choose a relay rated for the dust collector's horsepower and voltage. The Grainger 3A355 is suitable for a 1-hp collector running on 115 volts or a 2-hp unit running on 230 volts. For a 3-hp dust collector, choose a heavier relay (Grainger part no. 6C913).

PVC Pipe Dangers Debunked

Sparks Are Unlikely in 4-in.-dia. PVC Pipe

BY ROD COLE

Home-shop dust-collection systems have become increasingly popular, but their safety has been hotly debated. The primary issue is whether PVC pipe is safe for use as ductwork. Many claim that sparks in PVC pipe due to static electricity may ignite the dust cloud in the pipe. The specter of a giant fireball consuming a shop and home is repeatedly raised. Others claim you can ground PVC, thus ensuring its safety.

Two years ago I had to decide for myself: PVC or metal ducts for my basement shop. Being both an avid woodworker and a scientist, I made a concerted effort to understand the issues. Fortunately, I have the resources of the library at the Massachusetts Institute of Technology (MIT)^{SM} and a professor just down the hall who's an expert in the physics of lightning.

I studied static discharge from insulators, as well as the more general topic of dust ignition. I found that it's extremely unlikely for a home-shop-sized system to have a dust-cloud explosion. Commercial-sized systems have had dust-cloud explosions, but different phenomena come into play in larger systems, and 4-in.-dia. PVC is too small for use in such systems, where the airflow is much greater than in a home shop.

Sparks Are Unlikely in 4-in.-dia. PVC Pipe

In my research I turned to the *Journal of Electrostatics*, a publication that covers the effects and interactions of static electricity, particularly in commercial applications. This journal has published a number of studies on the combustibility of dust clouds by electrostatic sparks. The researchers were able to determine some of the conditions necessary to create sparks and ignite a dust cloud.

Sparks can be caused by a variety of conditions—one of which is static electricity. However, sparks are unlikely inside a standard 4-in.-dia. PVC pipe that would be used in a home shop, and, more important, any such sparks are extremely unlikely to be strong enough to cause an ignition. I can't say it is truly impossible, but it is very close to impossible, and I do not know of a single instance.

The difference between metal and PVC is that one is a conductor (metal) and the other is an insulator (PVC). A conductor allows electrical charges to flow freely. If any excess charge is not given a path to ground, it can arc, creating a spark that in certain conditions can ignite a flammable substance such as dust. Grounding provides a path for this excess charge to flow harmlessly to the earth, which is why dust-collection systems

in all commercial shops are required by code to be grounded. However, an insulator is a very poor conductor of electricity. While it's possible to get a static shock from the outside of a PVC pipe, it is highly unlikely for sparks to occur inside.

Dust Collectors with 3 hp or Less Pose Little Danger

I published my findings on my Web site. Rob Witter, a representative at Oneida Air Systems, Inc., which makes dust-collection systems, said he largely agreed with my research. "We as a company have been trying to trim away at these misunderstandings for years," he said. He added that plastic pipe will "probably never cause a problem" in a home shop. Finally, he pointed out that the National Fire

Real Small-Shop Fire Hazards

The static electric charge that builds up in 4-in.-dia. PVC pipe is not a hazard. But there are other dangers associated with sawdust.

BUILDUP OF DUST IN MACHINES. Hot metal that finds its way to the dust that collects at the base of a saw could start a fire there or be sucked up into the dust-collection system.

Protection Association (NFPA)[SM] puts no regulations on dust-collection systems of 1,500 cubic feet per minute (cfm) or less.

All of this discussion applies to home-shop-scale systems. Larger systems, complete with ducts and filters that move more than 1,500 cfm, require at least 3 hp and are not found in most home shops. Larger systems need larger ducts, and with that you have to begin to worry about more complicated forms of static sparks.

The Real Hazards

In a home shop, the dust-collection fire hazards you need to worry about are not in the ductwork but in the collection bag or bin itself. A fire may be caused by a spark, which can occur when a piece of metal is sucked into the ductwork and strikes another piece of metal, or by embers from a pinched blade. The spark or ember settles into the dust pile to smolder, erupting into a full-blown fire hours later, often after the shop has been shut down and no one is there to respond. For this reason, my most important recommendation is to empty the collected dust every day or at least keep it in a closed metal container.

As you can see from the photo of my shop, I ended up plumbing it using 4-in.-dia. PVC pipes and did not ground them. I feel perfectly safe using them this way.

ROD COLE is a woodworker and mathematician who lives in Lexington, Massachusetts. An expanded version of his research can be found at: gis.net/~dheaton/woodworking/woodworking.shtml.

CUTTING A NAIL. Not only does this damage a blade, but it can also send a very hot piece of metal into your saw cabinet.

SPARKS IN THE BAG. Metal sucked into the dust collector's fan blade may cause a spark and ignite sawdust in the filter bag.

METAL IN THE DUST PILE. When cleaning shop, it's easy to sweep up screws, washers, and nails. Dust from the floor should be sifted by hand, before it's introduced into a dust-collection system.

Woodworkers' First Aid

BY ALAN MARCO, M.D

Woodworking is inherently dangerous. It says so right on the copyright page of this book. It's the sort of thing everyone knows. I could begin with the story of John Woodough who loses a finger on a tablesaw, but that won't tell you anything you don't already know. What I want to tell you is what to do in the event of an accident: those cases when you can take care of yourself at home and those times when you need to get to the hospital. Being prepared might save an eye, a finger, or a lot of blood. And knowing what to do immediately after an accident can help those in the emergency room put you back together.

Minor Cuts and Abrasions

Cleanliness is a relative term. A clean woodshop is still a veritable petri dish of germs and dirt. Barring a serious laceration or amputation, you have to clean any bleeding injury with soap and water to ward off possible infection. Inspect your wound for foreign bodies. If it didn't grow in you, it's a foreign body: bits of wood, grit, metal. Remove them by flushing with water. For deeply imbedded grit, you may need to grit your teeth and use a scrub brush. Avoid alcohol or peroxide because both may cause more tissue irritation. To

kill germs, it's better to use a providone-iodine solution, available under many different brand names, such as Betadine®. Soap and water works too. Apply an antibiotic ointment to the wound if desired. If bleeding persists, apply pressure to the affected site with a clean gauze pad. When the bleeding stops, cover the small cut or abrasion with a dry, sterile bandage for two to three days.

Check the wound periodically for renewed bleeding or signs of infection, such as increased pain, swelling, or redness. Minor swelling and redness is normal in the first day or two. Also watch for red streaks going up your arm or leg or pus drainage. If these occur, you should have the injury evaluated by your doctor. If you have a serious medical condition such as diabetes, which can interfere with healing, you may want to have the wound checked by your doctor. Also, if your last tetanus vaccination was more than 10 years ago, get a booster shot at your next checkup.

For Serious Injuries: Don't Panic

Pain is your body's way of telling you something is wrong. And, fortunately, the body's immediate reaction to pain—roughly the amount of time between flip-

First-Aid Kit for Your Shop

Don't take supplies from your first-aid kit for anything other than treating accidents. Someday you might need the adhesive tape and scissors for an emergency only to remember you used them to pack up saw-blades to send out for sharpening. If you must use some of the supplies, replace them as soon as possible. Be aware of expiration dates on some first-aid supplies. This wall-mounted metal box is available from Lab Safety Supply℠.

TOP SHELF: An asthma inhaler can counteract allergic reactions to fumes and to exotic-wood dust; sharp scissors for cutting bandages; adhesive tape for bandaging; an elastic bandage for securing dressings.

MIDDLE SHELF: Needles for splinter removal are stored in sterile alcohol; splinter tweezers, precise enough to pick up a single hair; 4-in. by 4-in. gauze pads for bandaging; assorted adhesive strips for small boo-boos; clean plastic bag for amputated parts; sterile rolled gauze for bandaging; butterfly bandages for drawing together larger lacerations.

BOTTOM SHELF: Providone-iodine solution for killing germs; eye wash and cup; small mirror for eye inspections; instant ice packs to reduce swelling or for transporting amputated parts to the hospital; latex gloves for eye examinations.

ping a light switch and the light going on—is to remove itself from the offending situation.

The majority of woodworking injuries happen to the hands. The natural reaction when you've hurt your hand is to cover it with your other hand, put pressure on the wound and hold both hands to your stomach. But at some point, you have to look at what has happened. Of course it hurts, but

jumping up and down, yelling words that used to get your mouth washed out with soap, isn't going to help. Sit down and take a few deep breaths. Sitting down is a good idea for several reasons. It will tend to make you relax, as will the deep breaths, and if looking at the injury is going to cause you to swoon or feel light-headed, you're less likely to fall down from a seated position. Now, take a look at what has happened.

ABRASIONS AND SMALL CUTS:

Clean wound with soap and water. Apply antibiotic cream or providone-iodine solution. Bandage and check dressing daily. See your doctor if there are signs of infection: increased redness, pus, or red lines running from wound.

SPLINTERS:

Remove with sharp, pointed tweezers. (They should be sharp enough to pick up a single hair.) If splinter is completely under the skin, expose splinter end with sewing needle doused in alcohol, and then remove with tweezers.

LACERATIONS:

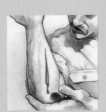

Clean wound with soap and water. Assess damage: If laceration is gaping or more than ¼-in. deep, seek emergency help. Otherwise, apply pressure to stop bleeding. Close wound with butterfly closures or adhesive strips. Check dressing daily.

FRACTURES:

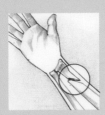

Signs include extreme pain, swelling, bruising, and an inability to move an adjacent joint. If you have any of these signs, you should be seen by a doctor to see whether you need an X-ray to evaluate for a fracture.

AMPUTATIONS:

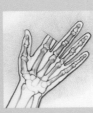

Apply pressure to wounded area with clean bandage. Don't panic. Call for help. Raise wounded area above heart. Wrap amputated appendage in plastic bag. Keep appendage cool, not directly on ice. Sit in a chair near door, and await help.

EYE INJURIES:

Look in mirror to assess eye. If foreign matter is embedded in the eye, go to the emergency room. If foreign matter is on the surface, flush it with water, or use eye wash and cup. For chemical splashes, flush with running water for 5 to 10 minutes. If it hurts too much to open your eye, go to the emergency room.

FUMES AND DUST:

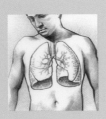

If you feel dizzy or are having trouble breathing, leave the area and go to fresh air. If normal breathing doesn't return in 15 minutes, go to the emergency room.

Lacerations In addition to the general guidelines given above, you should assess whether a laceration needs to be seen by a doctor. If the cut is spurting blood, there is likely to be an injury to an artery, and you should be seen in the emergency room. To control bleeding, apply pressure with a clean gauze pad. Apply an ice pack to reduce bleeding and pain.

If the bleeding is stopped or is minimal, inspect the wound. If the wound edges come together easily, clean the wound and apply a bandage. If the edges are somewhat separated, try to bring them together with butterfly closures or adhesive strips. If the laceration is gaping and more than ¼ in. deep—the edges do not come together—or if it is on your face, where scarring is less acceptable, you may need stitches. And go to a doctor if you see muscle (it looks like steak), fat, or tendons in the wound or if there is a flap of flesh.

If the area beyond the laceration is numb, you may have injured a nerve. If you cannot bend the adjacent joints, a tendon may have been injured. If the wound continues to spurt blood or the arm, leg, or finger is cold compared to the others, you may have injured the artery feeding that part, and you should go to the emergency room immediately.

Fractures The most likely fracture (i.e., a broken bone) woodworkers experience in the shop is a finger fracture, usually the result of a hammer or a nail gun. Shooting a nail through the bone in your finger is particularly serious because this type of broken bone, called an open fracture, has a high likelihood of infection.

How can you tell when a nail hits bone? Signs include extreme pain, swelling, and bruising. Although it may seem strange to list extreme pain, it's not to people who have done this. They have no problem distinguishing between hitting bone and just flesh. If a nail goes through a joint, get eval-

uated by a doctor. Another sign of a fracture is not being able to move the joint next to the injury because of pain. If you have any of these signs, go to a doctor to see whether you need an X-ray.

If you whack your finger with a hammer, put some ice on it. I stick my finger in a cup of water filled with ice cubes; it's easier than holding an ice pack. Check for the fracture signs given above, and if the finger isn't feeling better, have it checked by a doctor. A common thumb-whacking injury is a bruise under the fingernail; doctors call it a subungual hematoma. Although it looks terrible—and sounds terrible—it only needs draining if it causes such pain that you are unable to go about your business.

Amputations Let's face it—this is what we fear most. There's a scene in Ken Kesey's *Sometimes a Great Notion* where Hank Stamper pulls off his gloves, and his wife sees that he's cut off one of his fingers during work. Macho Hank just keeps working. She's horrified, and you should be too.

With any complete or partial amputation, the first step is to control bleeding with a pressure dressing. Wrap something clean around the wound, and hold on. Blood loss is a big factor here. An ice pack and elevating the affected site above the level of your heart will also help to control bleeding.

Amputations need professional attention, so proceed directly to the hospital. If you can find the amputated part, wash it off, place it in a plastic bag, and put the bag on ice. To avoid frostbite, do not put the part directly on ice. The doctors may not be able to reattach it, but the odds go way up if the amputated part is at the hospital and not in the sawdust bin back at the shop.

If you cut off more than a finger, immediately apply pressure to the stump to control bleeding. Don't panic; keeping cool can save your life. Call for help. If you can, unlock the front door to save time for the paramedics. Sit near the door or, if you feel light-headed,

Sources

Lab Safety Supply
800-356-0783
www.labsafety.com

lie on the floor. Don't worry about the cut-off part; the paramedics will find it.

Eye Injuries

The most common eye problems in the shop are from foreign bodies and chemicals. If you get something in your eye, don't poke at it with a dirty finger. Closely inspect the eye in a mirror or have someone do it for you. If the material is embedded in the eye, go to the hospital. If the material appears to be floating on the surface of the eyeball, the best thing is to flush it out with eye wash or plain tap water. Hold your eye open so that the water can actually wash out the material. The eye may not feel completely better because it may have been scratched, but if it is feeling better during the day, it should be fine. If the material is still in there, you should have a doctor examine the eye. Also, removing bits of metal should be left to a professional.

Chemical splashes from finishes or strippers can be very damaging to the eye. If a splash occurs, immediately flush the eye under running water for 5 to 10 minutes. If the eye is still painful or if an alkaline substance like lye, caustic strippers, or cement was splashed in the eye, you must be evaluated by a physician. As a general rule, if the eye hurts so much that you can't open it, go to a doctor at once.

Fumes and Dust

Breathing various fumes or dusts can cause illness. Some vapors from finishing products are heavier than air and will collect in our basement workshops unless vigorous efforts, such as exhaust fans and open windows, provide adequate ventilation. If you are working with a finish or solvent and feel dizzy or sleepy, you may be intoxicated by the vapors. Leave the area at once, opening a window or door to the outside as you go.

With the growing popularity and availability of exotic woods, comes an increasing incidence of allergic reactions. Repeated exposure to the oils in these woods can cause rashes, but it is possible for the allergy to first manifest itself by breathing problems such as acute asthma or wheezing. The fine dust or the smoke from machining these woods can trigger an attack. If you find that you are having trouble breathing while working with these woods, stop what you are doing, and leave the area. If you don't improve or are struggling to breathe—you can't get out more than a few words—you should seek medical attention. Over-the-counter asthma inhalers can be tried, but these may not be appropriate if you have high blood pressure or heart disease.

Also, woodworkers are at risk for chemical burns from some strippers that may contain lye or bleaching agents such as oxalic acid. If you come into contact with these materials, immediately flush the affected part with water for at least five minutes. If the area blisters, especially if it involves the face or hands, see a doctor.

What to Expect in the Emergency Room

Forget the television shows where the emergency room doctors and nurses are waiting to solve the day's problems in less than 50 minutes. Typically, you will be seen by the triage nurse who will determine the priority of your condition. Although a bad cut needing stitches is a big deal to you, it can wait while the patient having a heart attack is seen. Eventually, you will be seen by a doctor who will determine the extent of the injury and whether tests are needed, such as X-rays. If the injury is complex, such as full or partial amputation or severe eye injury, the emergency physician will arrange for consultation with the specialist on call, such as a hand surgeon, plastic surgeon, orthopedic surgeon, or ophthalmologist.

ALAN MARCO, M.D., is an anesthesiologist and a woodworker. His wife, Catherine Marco, M.D., an assistant professor of emergency medicine, assisted in writing this article.

Protect Your Hearing in the Shop

For nearly 20 years I was exposed to the often painfully loud whines of tablesaws and routers, banging hammers, whirring planers, and the assorted din you hear daily in a small cabinet shop. Did I wear hearing protection? Well, some of the time, but more often than not, no. I'd characterize those habits more as careless than as cavalier. I had two sets of earmuffs—one good pair for an employee and one fairly cheap set that I'd use on occasion. What I didn't like about those earmuffs was that they just weren't comfortable. The cushion quickly lost its spring and softness, affecting the seal; the plastic covering around the cushion was scratchy and hot, and it stuck to sweaty skin on warm days.

BY
WILLIAM DUCKWORTH

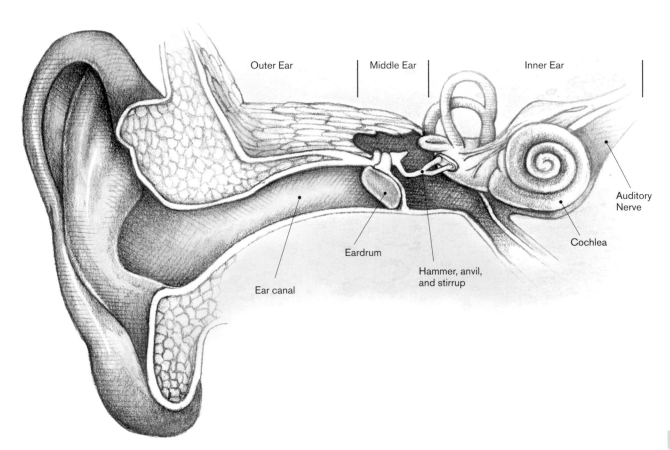

Outer Ear | Middle Ear | Inner Ear

Eardrum

Hammer, anvil, and stirrup

Ear canal

Auditory Nerve

Cochlea

How We Hear

The outer ear collects sound waves and directs them inward to the ear canal, which ends at the eardrum. A vibrating eardrum transmits sound waves to three small bones (hammer, anvil, and stirrup) in the middle ear that create mechanical vibrations within the fluid-filled cochlea in the inner ear. Extremely sensitive hair cells within the cochlea distribute the vibrations in the fluid to nerve fibers that create electrical impulses to carry the information to the brain via the auditory nerve.

THE INSIDE OF A NORMAL, HEALTHY COCHLEA contains thousands of cilia and hair cells that transmit sound vibrations. Noise damage causes hair cells to die, resulting in hearing loss.

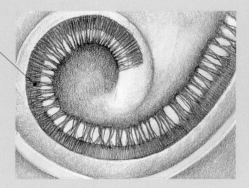

Healthy

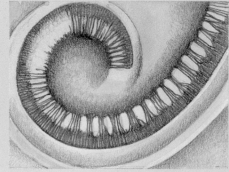

Damaged

After speaking with a number of people in the hearing conservation industry, from makers of protection devices to hearing-aid suppliers, it turns out that my experience was not uncommon. The biggest challenge many makers of hearing protectors face is making devices comfortable enough that people will actually use them. Another thing I learned is that the science behind the effort to provide good hearing protection can be quite complicated. But like most other fields of study, you don't have to understand all the science to benefit from its hard-won results. With that said, it may help to put some of that science into perspective.

Hearing Loss—What Is It, and What Causes It?

The onslaught of damaged hearing can result from medical problems, including illnesses. But the most common cause of damage is being too close to too much loud noise for too long. How much is too much?

Average daily noise levels of 80 decibels and lower pose no threat of hearing damage. Noise levels of 90 decibels and higher can be hazardous, and several machines in a woodshop exceed those levels (see the sidebar on the facing page). The duration of exposure has as much to do with it as the decibel level. Noise-induced damage is cumulatively degenerative and mostly irreversible.

Our outer ears collect sound (see the drawing on p. 125), directing it down the ear canal to the eardrum. Fluid in the inner ear conducts sound vibrations to the cochlea. The cochlea is to hearing what the retina is to seeing: Within each cochlea are approximately 35,000 tiny microscopic hairs, or cilia, that bend to the movements of fluid motions caused by the sound vibrations. The cilia connect to hair cells that set off nerve impulses that move through the auditory nerve to an area of the brain where the electrical messages translate into sounds the brain can recognize.

Shop Noise: How Loud Is It?

We set up a sound meter in the *Fine Woodworking* shop and took readings on machines and power tools running under load. We placed the meter on a tripod at ear level off the floor and placed it at a distance from the machines that would approximate an operator's position. Listed below are the decibel levels of the equipment we tested. Prolonged exposure to noises louder than 90 decibels poses the greatest threat.

DECIBEL LEVEL OF MACHINES

	75 dB	80 dB	85 dB	90 dB	95 dB	100 dB
Cordless Drill						
Planer						
Tablesaw						
Belt sander						
Router						
Shop Vacuum						

It is those cilia and hair cells that become the victims of noise-induced hearing loss. Repeated loud blasts of sound (air guns and hammer blows) or extended high-pitched whines (routers and belt sanders) can simply obliterate them or wear them out. And when those hair cells are destroyed and disappear, they don't grow back.

Noise-Reduction Ratings

Look at any package of earmuffs or disposable plugs, and you'll find a government-mandated noise-reduction rating (NRR),

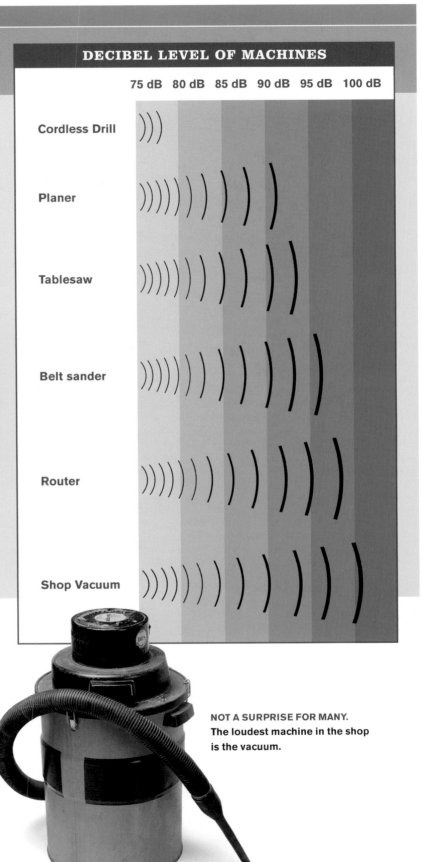

NOT A SURPRISE FOR MANY.
The loudest machine in the shop is the vacuum.

Plugs

There are many different types of hearing protection in the form of earplugs on the market. Many woodworkers have different preferences based on experience and the type of work they are doing at the time.

FOAM PLUGS

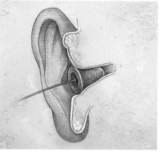

DEPRESS THE FOAM FIRS between your fingers, then pull up and back on the ear to insert the plug.

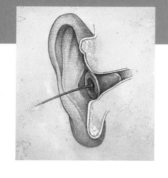

Disposable Foam Plugs

Learning to fit disposable foam plugs requires education. Inserted properly, foam plugs offer considerable protection.

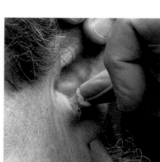

Reusable plugs

Barbed plugs are like toggle bolts: The soft plastic expands after being inserted into the ear canal. Hearing bands are convenient but offer the least amount of protection.

BARBED PLUGS

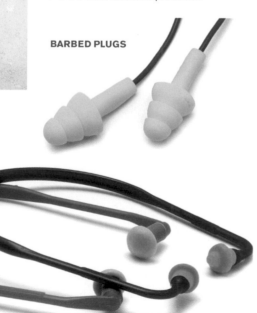

HEARING BANDS

which is an ideal laboratory measure. The NRR figure (usually in the teens or 20s) represents in decibels how much noise—on average across a spectrum of frequencies—that particular device will attenuate, or reduce. Lab technicians arrive at the figure by averaging the effects on at least 10 different people fitted with that device in a lab. Higher numbers signify greater effectiveness. However, in the real world these ratings don't mean a whole lot.

In the real world, people don't always fit themselves with a hearing-protection device correctly, as is often the case with plugs. One manufacturer I spoke with makes foam earplugs with an NRR of 29 decibels and a set of muffs with an NRR of 22 decibels. So I asked the scientist in the research and development lab whether I could then conclude that the foam plugs offered considerably better protection. The answer was a resounding no; as a matter of fact, the opposite is true. Earmuffs are relatively idiot-proof: You put them over your ears, and the spring action holds them firmly in place. Generic-sized foam plugs don't fit all ears the same, and many people simply don't know how to install them properly. So in the real world, the muffs usually offer better protection despite their lower rating.

And in the real world, people don't always use the device when they're exposed to noise. Is one quick cut on the tablesaw always worth a walk across the room to pick up that set of muffs you left on the workbench? One manufacturer suggested that for a more accurate and realistic assessment of how well a hearing-protection device will reduce sound within a workplace, you could roughly divide its NRR figure in half.

Many Types of Gear

Among the three or four major manufacturers of hearing protection devices, woodworkers have never been offered more choices than they have now. The two major categories of products offered—muffs and plugs—can be broken down into several subsets of hearing-protection devices (for a list of sources, please visit www.finewood-working.com).

Disposable Foam Plugs These things are surprisingly effective—as long as you learn how to fit yourself with them properly—and for about 20¢ a pair, you can't beat the price. We found one brand (Howard Leight Industries) with an NRR of 33 decibels. To fit them, it's important to insert them fully into the ear canal; otherwise, they won't offer much protection. Depress the foam by rolling it between your fingers. Pull back and up on your outer ear with one hand (which gives you better access to the ear canal) while inserting them with the other. As the foam begins to expand it sounds as though you've got an ear full of soda water for a few minutes until the foam fully regains it shape.

Foam plugs come with or without cords that hold a pair together. With the cord you're less likely to plop down the plugs on a workbench covered with sawdust.

Reusable Plugs and Hearing Bands Reusable plugs are made of soft plastic rather than foam. They're tapered and have successively larger barbed rings of the flexible plastic, which block off the ear canal. A hearing band is worn under the chin instead of over the head. The spring action of the plastic band holds two foam pads in place. But the pads cover only the outside of the ear canal, so they offer the least amount of protection of all of the devices I examined.

It actually hurt to wear the reusable plugs. The hearing band was just the opposite— comfortable and convenient. The NRR for the hearing band is low (20, 21 decibels), so it wouldn't be my first choice for protection from really loud noises. But when you're putting on hearing protection and taking it off repeatedly, there is something to be said for the convenience of leaving the band hanging around your neck. Also, you can wear the band and a set of safety

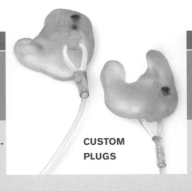

Custom-Made Earplugs

In the price range of $65 to $80, custom-fitted plugs are the most expensive alternative for plug-type protection. You can get plugs made with a filtered air channel (that facilitates conversation while wearing them) that offer protection with an NRR of 25 decibels to 29 decibels. Custom plugs without the air channel are rated as high as 37 decibels. You know these plugs will fit perfectly because they are made from a mold of each of your ears. To have a set made, look in your local yellow pages for a certified hearing specialist or a hearing-aid supplier.

CUSTOM PLUGS

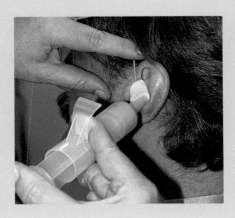

CUSTOM-FITTED PLUGS OFFER THE BEST FOR THE MOST. For people who already have damaged hearing or who simply want first-rate protection and don't mind paying for it, custom plugs can be the answer. Here, silicone is injected into the ear to make a mold.

glasses or goggles at the same time without compromising the hearing protection you are getting.

Muffs Among the various brands of muffs, you'll find a wide range of choices regarding cost and comfort. Surprise—the more expensive ones ($20 or more) are the most comfortable, but even the lower-priced versions (less than $10) are fairly cozy until they get too old and worn out. NRRs of muffs vary from as low as 15 decibels to as high as 33 decibels.

The one big downside with muffs is that you can't wear them with safety glasses without sacrificing their effectiveness because the stem of the glasses breaks the seal of the foam surrounding the ears. They also don't work well with full-face masks. You can

Sources

Howard Leight Industries
800-327-1110
www.howardleight.com
Aearo
800-225-9038
www.aearo.com

* Note that price estimates are from 2001.

Unusual Muffs for the Money

ADJUSTING THE VOLUME. The small foam pad on the bottom of the Leightning Pro Ears muff is a microphone. The volume control adjusts the noise level.

Here are two special exceptions to your standard foam-filled earmuffs. Leightning® Powered by Pro Ears®, made by Howard Leight Industries, are marketed primarily to gun users, who need protection from the loud impulse noise of shots being fired. Battery-powered electronics, small built-in microphones, and independent volume controls for each ear allow the person wearing these earmuffs to monitor conversations while loud noises are electronically compressed to safe levels. Wearing these muffs, you can still hear what goes on around you, but the noises don't hurt. At sporting-goods stores these muffs sell for about $250.

The Peltor® Lite-Com, made by Aearo®, is a wireless headset with a five-channel FM radio that has a communication range of more than 1,000 ft. The muffs connect to a transmitter/receiver, which is equipped with a belt clip. These muffs would work in a busy commercial or industrial shop, where workers face an all-day din. They might also work for the well-to-do home hobbyist who wants to keep in touch with a spouse in another part of the house. These units sell for about $300, and they are designed for extended wear.

KEEP IN TOUCH IN A BUSY SHOP. The Peltor Lite-Com headset, designed for daylong wear in noisy environments, makes it possible to communicate with others by way of a built-in radio.

MUFFS Muffs are the benchmark of the industry. Regular earmuffs range in cost from about $8 to $25, and have an NRR of 15 decibels to 33 decibels.

wear them with a set of goggles held in place with an elastic band, but many people don't like wearing goggles because they tend to fog up, obscuring good vision.

More than one industry source suggests a solution for people who have to face extended exposure to extremely loud environments or people who already have hearing damage and can't risk exacerbating it: Wearing both the foam plugs and earmuffs at the same time increases the level of hearing protection by about 6 decibels.

WILLIAM DUCKWORTH, associate editor of *Fine Woodworking* magazine, is a lucky man. A hearing specialist recently tested him and said that despite all that time spent in the shop he has "unbelievably good hearing."

Pain-Free Woodworking

BY THOMAS P. LEROY

How many times has this happened to you: You're bent over for two minutes, reaching under your router table to make that final depth adjustment. When you try to stand up—yeow!—it feels like a chisel has been stuck in your back. It's not just age; it can be a sign of cumulative trauma. Pain is a warning. Your back has just told you that the position you've worked in is a no-no. Keep it up, and someday the pain might not go away so fast.

I'm both a physical therapist and a member of the Guild of New Hampshire Woodworkers. Fellow members frequently tell me about aching backs, stiff necks, and sore shoulders. These injuries don't necessarily result from one specific incident, but rather they are often caused by prolonged overuse or misuse of your body. They are the proverbial piling on of straws that break the camel's back. These injuries can happen to any body part, and they can range in seriousness from a small annoyance that decreases your enjoyment of woodworking to a debilitation that keeps you away from your workbench for long periods of time. *Cumulative* is the key word here. (The advice that I give in this article has to be somewhat general. If you have specific, intense injuries, you should consult your doctor.)

Begin in Neutral

To understand how you can prevent cumulative trauma to your body while working, you will need to be comfortable with a few general concepts. First, each joint—where two or more bones meet—has a neutral position. This position exists roughly at the midway point between the joint's extremes of motion. When a joint is in neutral, it is in its least-stressed position. Think of a balanced seesaw, with the plank horizontal, a simplified paradigm of a joint in neutral. Turn your head as far to the right as you can and then to the left. Neutral position for your neck in this plane of motion is facing straight ahead, midway between extremes.

The farther a joint is out of neutral, the more stress there is on the joint surfaces, the surrounding muscles, and their tendons. The more time spent out of neutral also increases the load on these structures. Stress and load cause fatigue and, possibly, pain. These facts

Raise the Work

Cutting dovetails can be a pain in the neck. Canting your head forward to get your eyes closer to your work puts tremendous strain on your neck muscles (below left), leading to headaches and muscle pain. For backsaw cutting, the author made a jig that raises his work off the bench (below right), enabling him to stand straighter with his neck closer to neutral.

Wrong   **Right**

Or Lower Your Body

Have a seat. Don't bend forward to get a closer look at your work. This position (below left) puts a lot of stress on your back and neck. It's better to sit on a stool to bring your head and eyes closer to the work at hand. Sitting also allows your back and neck to remain in their neutral positions.

Wrong   **Right**

lead us to the second concept: To decrease the factors that can lead to cumulative trauma injuries (read: pain), you must spend more time closer to your neutral positions.

Often, mere awareness of proper work positions is not enough. Your overused muscles can get tight during a day in the shop. This creates a situation much like twist in a board that pulls it out of a true plane. Tightened muscles can pull joints farther out of neutral and make it difficult to modify how you work. For a simple stretching program that targets some of the major muscle groups of the shoulders, neck and back, see the sidebar on page 135.

Your Head Weighs 15 Lbs.

When you work wood, the primary function of the neck is to position your eyes so that you can use your hands. A problem arises because your eyes are encased in your head, which weighs about 15 lbs. The neutral position of the neck is ear hole over the shoulder. If you were to hold 15 lbs. in your hand close to your body and then hold your arm in front of you, you would quickly realize the greater effort needed to maintain the second position.

Now, realize that woodworkers won't be walking around shops with books balanced on their heads. I merely want you to lessen the stress on your neck whenever possible by staying closer to neutral position. Some early warning signs of too much nonneutral head-holding are fatigue in neck muscles, headaches centered around the base of your skull, or neck stiffness, especially in the morning. Because nerves pass through your neck, staying closer to neutral will also help protect your arms.

Would you try to thread a needle while holding it at waist level? I doubt it. Remember: Head position is intimately linked to vision. Dimly lit areas or lighting that casts shadows across work surfaces cause you to bring your eyes closer to the work and your neck farther out of neutral. Mobile task lighting is a simple, inexpensive solution.

Also, you can either lower your body toward the work or raise your work off the bench (see the sidebar on the facing page).

Because the neck and shoulder blades have some muscles in common, arm position can be another factor that leads to a forward head position. The more you reach away from your body—such as when spraying or hand-applying finish deep in a cabinet—the tendency increases to have your head forward from neutral. Tipping your head too to look up is painful, too. And if you have just started to use bifocals, be cautious about working with your head tipped back for prolonged periods of time.

Care for Your Shoulders

Your shoulders function to place your arms and hands where they are needed and provide force to move an object in your hands. The amazing trait of the shoulder is its mobility and range of motion. Compared to the hip, the shoulder is vastly more mobile; think of all of the places you can put your hands that you can't put your feet.

To be able to move as it does, the shoulder sacrifices stability; it is one of the joints most frequently dislocated. This makes the muscles that surround the shoulder responsible for not only moving the joint but also keeping the bones aligned properly. The rotator cuff—a term referring to four specific muscles—assists in the precise control needed to keep this mobile joint working properly. For the rotator cuff to function best, correct position of the shoulder blade is key.

Let's look at how common woodworking tasks can cause problems. Activities that involve using your hands close together—planing, scraping, routing, lathe work—can tighten chest muscles. This tightness tends to cause the shoulder blades to round forward, which in turn makes the rotator cuffs less efficient. You now have a situation in which every instance of lifting an arm causes a little damage, especially if heavy weight is involved or the hand is significantly above shoulder level.

Bend Your Knees, Not Your Back

Stand up straight, and you'll feel great. Bending over a router table for long periods of time can lead to an aching back. Bend at the waist and bend your knees to get closer to your work, but keep your back in neutral.

Wrong

Right

Careful planning of your shop can decrease the wear and tear on the shoulders and their muscles. Any heavy object—a jointer plane, a router—should be stored below shoulder level. Lighter objects can be kept higher, but I try to avoid placing frequently used objects above eye level no matter how little they weigh.

Limit the amount of time you spend with your arms overhead. This can lead to the rotator-cuff tendons rubbing against bone spurs. Finishing a tall piece or installing overhead ductwork for a dust-collection system are both examples of situations in which you should raise yourself up to the level of the task.

The Lower Back Is the Body's Keystone

Your lower back works as a stable base from which your arms and legs move and generate force. As in the neck, the neutral position is important. When viewed from the side, your back in neutral should have a slight curvature—convexity facing forward.

Keep Your Belt Parallel to the Floor

Don't cant your hips. If you stand at a bench for a long time, fatigue will make you cant your hips, leading to back pain. Try standing with one foot on something. When your belt is parallel to the floor, it's a good sign that your hips are straight.

Wrong

Right

It's helpful to envision two extremes: The Pink Panther® has a flat back with no curve, and Donald Duck's® back has excessive curve, rump feathers sticking out in the air. As is the case with most joints, the lower back's neutral position is roughly in the middle of the two. It's not just a matter of posture; you can incline your body far forward and still keep your back in neutral by hinging at the hips like a waiter's bow.

One of the most important concepts for long-term back safety is proper work-surface height. Different tasks require different heights. No one magical percentage of your inseam exists to determine what is best. Instead, choose a height that keeps you as close to neutral as possible while enabling you to work comfortably. Keep in mind that machine and bench manufacturers try to find a height that's fairly suitable for most people. Some of us have to raise the working heights, while others must lower them.

Just as in the shoulder and neck, a lower-back concern is spending too much time toward the extremes. Pain is a sign that you are overtaxing your lower back. An insidious cause of the opposite extreme—bending back for too long—can occur with prolonged standing. Once your trunk muscles fatigue, the hips often sway forward to gain stability by leaning against the bench or a countertop. To maintain balance the upper back leans back, which exaggerates the lower back's normal curvature. This can also happen when you're working on a ladder.

Additional suggestions don't require the modification of machinery or the building of jigs. A cluttered shop increases the chance that you'll bend improperly or reach excessively. Also, pay attention to your feet. They should point in the direction your center of gravity is moving. Woodworkers often do this reflexively when hand-planing or ripping a board on the tablesaw. This allows us to shift weight from the back foot to the front and use the large muscles of the leg to do the work. When standing for long periods of time, it is common to shift more weight on one foot than on another. This is okay as long as you don't bend the unweighted knee so much as to allow that side of your pelvis to drop (see the photos on p. 134).

To conclude, be aware of how you move and position yourself. Whenever possible, try to stay closer to those neutral positions. It may seem awkward at first, but relearning correct positions will help avoid pain. Also, the old cliché about variety being the spice of life applies: Even while doing the same activity, try to introduce some variability. Be creative; build a jig or modify a task, get a comfortable stool. And if you start to hurt, take a break and stretch. The body you save will be your own.

THOMAS P. LEROY is a physical therapist and woodworker in Chester, N.H.

Stretch It Out

Less than five minutes—that's how long these exercises take to stretch and loosen up your muscles. That's less time than it takes to sharpen a chisel. You wouldn't think of starting work with a dull chisel, and you shouldn't think of starting work with tight muscles.

Hold each of these stretches for 15 seconds (except where noted), and do each one for three repetitions. Remember that you're stretching, not really pushing or pulling. And never bounce your way into a stretch. Slow and easy. You'll feel your tight muscles, and as you hold the stretch, you'll feel them loosen a little. You can do these exercises any time during the day if you start to feel stiffness or pain. You'll feel better and, possibly, be able to work a longer day.

SHOULDER STRETCH. This stretch will loosen your chest muscles. Place your hands on both sides of a doorway, a little above shoulder level. Step into the doorway with one foot. Shift your weight onto the forward foot, leaning into the doorway, keeping your back straight. Hold for 15 seconds. Repeat two more times.

HAMSTRING STRETCH. Place your heel on a low stool. While keeping your knee and your back straight, lean forward at the hips. You'll feel the muscles in the back of your thigh stretch. Hold for 15 seconds. Now do the same thing with your other leg. Repeat two more times for each leg.

NECK SIDE STRETCH. Rest your right hand behind your back to keep your shoulder down. With your left hand on top of your head, tilt your head toward the left. Make sure your neck is straight, not canted forward or backward. Hold for 15 seconds. Now do the same thing to the right. Repeat two more times in each direction.

STANDING BACK STRETCH. This is an excellent stretch after being bent forward for a long time. Keeping your knees straight, bend backward at the waist. Hold for five to 10 seconds. Repeat two more times.

BACKWARD NECK STRETCH. Without tipping your head, bring your head straight back so that your ears are directly over your shoulders. Hold for 15 seconds. Repeat two more times.

Basement Shop on Wheels

BY ANATOLE BURKIN

My first shop was an old garage nestled on a bank above Puget Sound near Seattle. It had an old plank floor with gaps wide enough to swallow small tools and hardware. For power I had one extension cord that snaked back to the house, and lighting was provided by an open garage door. I have fond memories of that shop, bundled up against the cold, working under natural light, hacking away and successfully cutting my first dovetail joint. I remind myself of those days when confronted by the limitations of my current shop, which by comparison is a dream.

My basement shop is only 20 ft. by 21 ft.—about the size of a two-car garage—but I've tackled projects as large as a run of kitchen cabinets. The secret to getting the most out of this small space is mobility. Almost everything rests on locking casters—machines, tables, and shop-built tool chests.

Storage and organization are also vital in a small space. The area under every machine tool or bench is utilized for storage. Yes, it does get crowded when I undertake a large project. But I can reconfigure the space as needed for milling, assembling, and finishing.

Convertible Shop

A small shop can't be all things at all times. Design it with adaptability in mind.

1. A roller, clamped to the bed of the jointer, which is placed close to the tablesaw, helps support wide stock for crosscutting.

2. To gain space in the center of the shop for assembly, the jointer may be moved.

3. The outfeed table wheels away to create a finishing area.

4. In preparation for spraying, a drop cloth is tossed over machines.

5. A wooden duct extension fits between the shopmade air cleaner and window frame to exhaust overspray.

6. The fine-particle filter has been replaced with a coarse furnace filter to capture finish before it blows outdoors.

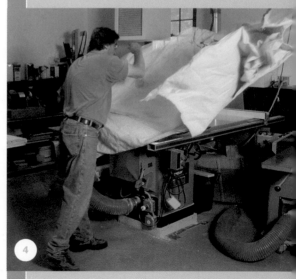

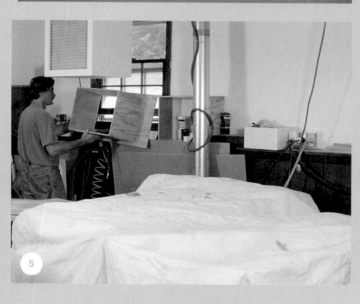

Layout for a Small Shop

Some tools are best left stationary. My tablesaw stays put because it's bulky and heavy. And the dust collector must have a permanent home because of the metal ductwork attached to it. The rest of the shop was designed to work around these machines.

Machine tools, as well as benches, must be located where they can handle the largest piece of stock I am likely to use. And with a small dust collector, I have to keep duct runs to a minimum. I try to keep most of the mobile tools parked where they can be put into service easily.

In a small shop, you'll often see the tablesaw angled. This orientation takes advantage of the room's diagonal dimensions. That's a good solution, but it typically means the saw reaches into the center of the room. When I have a large project going, such as a run of cabinets, I like having the center of the shop available for assembly. I orient the tablesaw parallel and close to the shop's longest wall, which

In a crowded space, adjoining tools can be set up to work with, not hinder, one another.

leaves me with more than enough room to cut a full sheet of plywood. The tablesaw's outfeed table is set on casters so I can wheel it out of the way and use that space for spray finishing.

In a crowded space, adjoining tools can be set up to work with, not hinder, one another. Although I'd like to have a sliding table for my tablesaw, I haven't the space. But I use my 8-in. jointer, which is parked to the left of the saw, to assist with sheet goods. At a scrap metal yard I picked up a set of metal rollers from a conveyor assembly. I made a wooden frame for the roller that allows it to be clamped to the jointer bed and provides support when handling sheet goods. Total outlay was about $2.

The jointer-tablesaw pairing didn't work at first because the jointer fence was higher than the tabletop of the saw. Lowering the jointer seemed like a lot of work, so I raised the tablesaw on blocks. It turns out that the added height has made repetitive tasks, such as tenoning, much more comfortable for my 6-ft. frame.

SAWDUST IS CAPTURED BY A BOX, which is connected to the dust collector. A roller bolted to the left of the table provides stock support. The workbench (with the aid of a piece of scrap) provides support to the right of the chopsaw.

Plenty of Room for the Chopsaw

Although the chopsaw is small, it's called on to handle very long stock. Finding the perfect spot was a compromise. There isn't room for a dedicated chopsaw stand with 8-ft.-long wings on both sides, so I use my European-style workbench to serve as one wing. A piece of scrap laid across the table serves as a low-tech outfeed support. To the left of the chopsaw, I use another one of those scrap-yard conveyor rollers to make it easy to slide stock into place.

Chopsaws spray sawdust all over the place, and while I haven't totally solved the problem, my method works okay. The key component is a capture box behind the saw to catch dust that's kicked back. A 5-in. port is added to the top of the box and connects to my dust-collection system. Additionally, I run a small hose from the saw's dust port (where the bag goes) and snake it a few inches into the 5-in. dust-collector hose. Whatever doesn't go up the hoses eventually settles into the capture box.

Thicknessing Machines

I have more thicknessing machines than I really have a right to own, but I've figured out a way to keep them from being a nuisance. For taking a thin pass or thicknessing highly figured woods, nothing beats a portable thickness planer with rubber infeed and outfeed rollers. Bigger machines, such as my 15-in. thickness planer, are good for hogging off material, not delicate passes. And when it comes to removing tearout from highly figured woods or sanding shopmade veneer, I appreciate every penny I spent on my drum-style thickness sander.

Because I only use one of these tools at a time, I have one dust hose hanging from the ceiling to serve them all. To save space, I mounted the small planer piggyback on the larger one. Although the portable unit can be lifted off and placed on a bench, I typi-

cally just leave it in place and plane boards at chest height. Below the planer and sander I've installed shelving to store sanding belts and other tools.

A Simple, Functional Router Table

My router table has evolved over the years. It now features dust collection above and below, bit storage, and a top large enough to hold a second router.

The dust collection might not meet the highest possible standards, but I'm happy with it. A large reducer (10 in. to 5 in.) is set into the base of the cabinet and connects to the dust collector. On

MACHINES TO SURFACE STOCK.
A 15-in. planer can remove stock quickly. The benchtop planer riding piggyback excels at taking light passes without leaving knife marks. And a drum sander (not shown) speeds up what most consider the least enjoyable part of woodworking.

top, the fence has a port for a 2½-in.-dia. hose. A pair of doors allows easy access to the router. The cabinet is set on wheels so that it can be moved to a corner when not in use.

Places to Store Tools

I have a small, simple tool rack near my workbench in which I keep chisels, handsaws, mallets, and hammers. The workbench has two shelves to store all of the handplanes I own. Now that the shelves are full, I know I have enough of them.

Most other small tools are kept in mobile shop-built carts. One houses everything I own for drilling and screwing. Most of the time it sits next to the drill press, but when I'm assembling parts, I roll the cart to where I'm working. The other cart contains measuring tools as well as all-around stuff, such as mechanic's wrenches and drivers. Both carts can also serve as stock carriers, for moving parts from one machine to another. (The mobile router table can also be used this way.)

Storage and organization are vital in a small space. The area under every machine tool or bench is utilized for storage.

The idea of putting all of my clamps in a trash can isn't new. But to keep the long pipe clamps from tipping over the can, I built a simple rack that is screwed into the can and keeps the clamps more or less upright. The can is mounted on a dolly, so I can move it around.

Low-Cost Electrics and Pneumatics

I originally lit my shop using cheap shop-light fixtures that cost about $7 apiece and that worked out to about a buck a year before they began failing. I recently swapped them with flush-mount fixtures of a higher quality that have electronic ballasts, which are quieter and turn on instantly. The fixtures also use T-8 bulbs, which are more energy efficient. I connected them using a plastic track system that is compact and easy to install. Most home centers sell these fixtures, and it's an inexpensive way for a non-electrician to set up a satisfactory lighting system. I spent about $250 for the five fixtures and hardware.

The shop did not have 240-volt power when I moved in. To keep down costs, I went with PVC conduit, installed on the rear outside wall of the house. Then I routed enough wire through the conduit to give me a gang of three 240-volt circuits. A 12-gauge extension cord, snaked along the main dust-collection duct, brings 240-volt power to the middle of the shop.

I find a lot of uses for compressed air: everything from pneumatic tools to clearing out dust from wood pores before spray finishing. I didn't want to go to the trouble of plumbing my shop, but at the same time I didn't want just one large coil of hose to drag from one part of the shop to the other. The solution is a three-in-one manifold and filter that allows me to provide clean, dry air to three locations both inexpensively and quickly. One long hose runs out to the garage. Another long one snakes along the ductwork and provides air to the opposite side of the shop. Near the compressor, a short run of hose provides air for spray finishing.

Spray Finishing without a Booth

I like to spray finish. You can't beat a spray gun for speed and the amount of control it brings to the task. But I don't have room for a spray booth. Nonetheless, I can spray in the shop without worrying about dust specks by using a two-pronged approach. First, I clean the shop before finishing. I'm not overly fussy about the cleanup except in the corner where I spray. Second, I use fast-drying finishes, such as water-based products or shellac. I don't spray slow-drying or highly flammable finishes.

Spray finishing also requires a method of removing the overspray. I installed a large industrial fan in a box made of medium-density fiberboard (MDF) and hung it in front of a window. When I spray, I open the window and press-fit an extension duct to the fan box, which helps direct the air outdoors without fouling the window casing. The fan box has a slot for a coarse furnace filter in front, which catches much of the finish before it reaches the fan. Without the extension duct in place, the fan doubles as an air cleaner. For that application, I use a fine-particle filter. (In warm weather, one could just flush the air outdoors.)

The tablesaw outfeed table doubles as my spray-finish bench for small objects. To keep it and the saw clean, I cover the entire setup with a large drop cloth. For larger pieces, I unclamp the outfeed table from the saw and roll it out of the way. And to keep finish off the walls and floor, I keep on hand large pieces of cardboard, such as those used to package appliances.

A Shop Is Never Done

I've been itching to get my hands on an old lathe but haven't found one yet. In the meantime, I've rearranged the shop in my head a number of times to make room for a newcomer. Try as I might, I'm not sure I can fit one more large tool in that space.

Which leaves me thinking that maybe it's time to consider a freestanding building or moving to another location with the sort of shop space everyone craves: a large barn with a loft. I could get a few hundred bucks selling all of the used casters, enough to buy a nice, new handplane. But until then, I'll enjoy the space I have.

ANATOLE BURKIN is the executive editor of *Fine Woodworking* magazine.

CLAMPS TO GO. Stored in a metal trash can, clamps can be wheeled to the assembly area, then rolled into an out-of-the way corner when not needed.

Woodworking Benches

BY MICHAEL DUNBAR

LOW BENCH FOR HANDWORK.
Planing moldings, chopping mortises, and jointing boards all require lots of upper-body strength. A low bench–the one in the photo is 31 in. high– allows the author to put a lot of muscle into his motions.

It is almost impossible to work wood without a workbench. It ranks as one of the most important fixtures in a shop. In fact, the more extensive your woodworking experience the more likely you are to have more than one bench. I have always had at least three benches in my chair-making school's shop—large and small joiner's benches and an assembly bench.

Different Benches, Similar Qualities

Different types of woodworkers traditionally have had different styles of benches that vary according to the needs of their craft. For example, a joiner's bench is long and narrow with a vise along the side (known as a side vise) and a vise at one end (known as a tail vise). Chair makers frequently work on a low platform called a framing bench

because chair assembly is called framing. All good benches share features you will want to include in any bench you are making or acquiring.

A Strong Bench Is Dependable A bench must be sturdy. You frequently place a lot of weight on it. Woodworking, especially with hand tools, creates a lot of force. A bench that wobbles or racks under these forces is frustrating to work on because you waste a lot of energy moving the benchtop rather than working wood. Also, this type of movement is not good for the bench's joints. They wear more quickly, and you may need to replace the bench down the road.

All the benches in my shop have 4x4 legs, and the stretchers are joined with 2-in.-deep mortise-and-tenon joints. The top is secured to 2x6 cleats that are mortised to sit on tenons cut into the top of the legs. We have reinforced all the multiple-person benches with cross-bracing—both end to end and side to side.

Heavy Benches Stay Put A bench should also be heavy. The forces exerted on a bench can not only rack it but also make it slide around the shop. Chasing your bench while trying to work wood is very frustrating. A heavy bench is more likely to stay put. A thick top is one way to create weight. The top of my large joiner's bench (see the photo on the facing page) is 2½-in.-thick beech, and all of our multiple-person benches (see the photo above) require four people to lift them safely.

Storing some of your tools under the bench is another good way to add weight. I store my working handplanes, about 20 of them, on a shelf that spans the side stretchers.

You can also secure the bench to the floor to keep it from moving. My small joiner's bench is lagged to the wooden floor. If you have a concrete floor, you may need to drill holes in it and use lag shields.

HIGH BENCH FOR MACHINING. Benchtop machines come with their own horsepower, so the operator's strength is almost superfluous. Slipping battens under the plywood has raised the actual working height of the benchtop to almost 36 in. Adding height is easy; lowering it isn't.

GET THE HEIGHT JUST RIGHT. To determine the proper workbench height, stand with your arm hanging by your side. Bend your wrist so that your palm is facing down.

In this case, be sure to locate the bench in the most desirable location.

Chair making requires a lot of shaping. When a student would pull the draw knife, the bench would follow. We corrected this by placing cleats against the legs and screwing them to the floor. And the cleats have another advantage. Although low—only ¾ in. thick—they keep a lot of the shavings produced in the shop from working their way under the bench, making clean up easier.

Your bench should be sized appropriately to your work. A benchtop has three impor-

AN IMMOVABLE BEAST. **To keep his benches from racking, the author uses dovetailed diagonal braces. Cleats screwed to the floor prevent the benches from moving.**

tant dimensions: length, width, and height. If you work with long pieces of wood, you want a long bench. When I built my joiner's bench, I was doing a lot of house restoration. As a result, I was making a lot of doors and interior and exterior trim. The 8-ft.-long top came in handy for this work.

Bench Width and Height A bench should be wide enough to handle the jobs you normally do. My joiner's bench is 32 in. wide. This is sufficient for most of the chairs, tables, or carcases I have built.

Bench height is perhaps the most critical dimension. It is one that is also very personal. It varies depending on your methods of work and your height. In a production shop where parts are mostly machined, benches are generally used for assembly. These benches tend to have higher working surfaces. However, a high bench makes working by hand very difficult. For example, when planing, you use muscles in your legs and back. On a high bench, you are more limited to your arm and shoulder muscles. I do a lot of handwork, and for that reason, I prefer a low bench. My large joiner's bench is only 31 in. high.

To determine bench height, stand erect with your arm hanging by your side, and bend your wrist so your palm is facing down. This is a good height for your bench. If you do a lot of work with benchtop machines, such as a router or a biscuit joiner, you may want the bench slightly higher. Remember this: It's easy to add temporary blocks or battens if you want to raise the working height of a bench for a particular project, but it's awfully hard to lower it.

MICHAEL DUNBAR is a contributing editor to *Fine Woodworking* magazine.

Vises Are a Woodworker's Third Hand

I have watched a lot of frustrated beginning woodworkers attempt to saw a piece of wood while holding it against a workbench with their free hand or their knee. I even saw one diligent guy put a board on a workbench, then sit on the board while he tried to make a cut. Pity that all of them didn't clamp their work in a vise.

Vises are indispensable woodworking tools. Through the day, a woodworker has to hold any number of things, such as parts or tools, so that he can work on them.

A Variety of Vises

Different styles of vises are made for a variety of different purposes. Thus, the longer you work wood, the more likely you are to own more than one vise. I started with one and now have six.

Vises are commonly built into woodworkers' workbenches. A typical joiner's bench has two—a side vise and a tail vise. A side vise is usually mounted along the length of a bench and is generally used for holding boards or parts on their edges. Holding a board for jointing with a handplane is a common job for the side vise. A tail vise—usually mounted on the end of a bench—holds boards or parts flat on the benchtop (see the photo at left). It is generally used in conjunction with benchdogs.

BY MICHAEL DUNBAR

A TAIL VISE IS FOR WORKING WOOD FLAT ON THE BENCH. Chopping mortises, face-planing or sanding is easy with a tail vise mounted so that the screw is parallel to the bench's length. The vise clamps the wood against a benchdog, the movable square peg at the front end of the new wood.

Planing or sanding a board's face and gluing panels are common jobs that involve the tail vise.

In my chair-making school's shop, we use two other types of vises on a daily basis. My favorite, the carriage vise, is similar to a machinist's vise but is made to much more exacting tolerances. It was manufactured early this century by the Prentise Vise Co™. In the company's catalog, this model is listed as a "woodworker's vise," but it is intended more specifically for carriage makers.

The jaws are at chest level, making it easier to work in a standing position, which is especially helpful for fine work. The jaws' faces are machined flat so that they do not mar the work, even when it is held very tightly. The screw has little backlash, so I can tighten and loosen the jaws with a half twist. I have had the Prentise carriage-maker's vise for 27 years. It serves me as a third hand, and without it, I would feel lost.

The other type of vise used in our shop is the Record 53E. This model is so well known and so widely used by woodworkers everywhere that it is the standard add-on cast-iron bench vise.

A once-popular type, pattern-maker's vises were made in large numbers and can still be found (though they're expensive). Pattern makers worked with irregular shapes and frequently needed to revolve the work to place it in an advantageous posi-tion. Their vises were far more flexible and complicated than those used by other branches of woodworking. Veritas® makes a modern version of a pattern-maker's vise called the Tucker Vise.

Use a Vise to Your Advantage

When I visit other shops or watch students at work, I observe two common problems. Many woodworkers use vises that are inade-quate, or they frequently do not use their vises to their best advantage. Whatever type of vise or vises are required in your work, they should all be high quality and strong. It is also usually a good bet to buy a brand you recognize. You will not be well served by a lightweight or undersized vise. Acquiring a good vise usually means spending the long dollar. However, the investment will pay dividends for as long as you work wood.

Using a vise to its best advantage is a regular part of our classroom instruction. It is easier to work wood if it is securely held by the vise. But avoid working in a way that allows the part to flex. It is usually best to lower the wood you are working on as far into the vise as possible so that it doesn't project a lot. Try to keep the area you are working as close to the jaws as possible to keep the workpiece rigid.

It doesn't matter whether the waste or the piece you are keeping gets clamped into the vise—whatever holds better is best. For instance, if you are cutting the waste off the end of a turned spindle, which would be

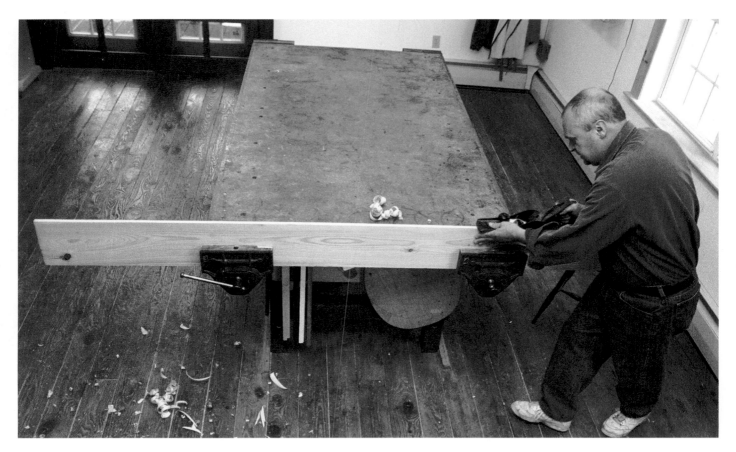

hard to clamp securely because of the turnings, it will be easier to clamp the waste piece in the vise and hold the spindle in your hand as you saw with your other hand. And if you have to joint pieces too small to run across a jointer, clamp a #7 jointer plane upside down in a vise and push the piece over it.

With a little forethought, vises can be adapted to better suit your needs. In our school, we cannot provide each student with several types of vises, so we have mounted Record 53E vises in a versatile way that allows them to perform all the jobs we require, such as holding chair seats for planing, turned legs for drilling, or spindles for shaping. Many shops mount a bench vise on the bench's long edge and set it in from the corner. Ours are located on the bench's short end and right on the corner. This allows us to use them as a tail vise for planing. A row of dog holes is aligned with the vise's dog (which is mounted in

SIDE VISES ON THE END OF A BENCH. For his Windsor-chair-making classes, the author mounted two Record 53E vises on the short end of each bench (above), which allows him to work off the corner of the bench. Working the long edge of a board is easy with tandem-mounted vises.

SMOOTH OPERATOR. This antique Prentise vise (left) has smooth faces that won't mar wood.

the outside jaw). And when jointing very long pieces, we can clamp the wood using two vises on the end of a bench.

MICHAEL DUNBAR is a contributing editor to *Fine Woodworking* magazine.

A Woodworker's Apron

BY STEVE LATTA

MECHANICAL DRAFTING PENCIL Use 2mm lead size.

SCREWS Fill an old prescription bottle with screws of differing lengths for jig setups.

EARPLUGS Foam plugs are a good backup when your muffs are out of reach.

BIB-STYLE APRON The long front provides plenty of pockets for storage.

At the shop I apprenticed in, all of the cabinetmakers wore shop aprons. I soon figured out why, and my productivity took a giant leap forward. A lot less time got wasted chasing down misplaced tape measures, safety glasses, pencils, and the other basic essentials. Because the tools I needed most often were within immediate reach, the quality of my work improved as well. Today, I still wear an apron, even when I'm teaching, and I advise students to do likewise.

The size of your shop, its tooling, and the nature of your work will determine what tools find their way into your apron pockets. But for starters, I suggest stocking your apron with basic marking and measuring tools. I've chosen light, compact, and high-quality measuring tools. Among my favorite brands are Starrett®, Lufkin® and Lee Valley. My students often balk at the prices of top-end tools, such as the $75 Starrett adjustable bevel. But if you're going to do accurate work and carry around this stuff all day, choose tools built to high tolerances that are light in weight and bulk. In the long haul, you'll be glad you did.

Tools aren't the only items that belong in a shop apron. A lot of cabinetwork involves boring small holes and fitting screws for hinges and hardware, usually #6 or #8

sizes. Many jigs may also be constructed with screws. So I keep bits, drivers, and various screws on hand. Used prescription or film canisters make good storage devices for small items.

Years ago, I had a batch of five aprons custom made, because I prefer flaps on the upper pockets, which keep out most sawdust (and small squares from falling in front of spinning tablesaw blades), and shoulder straps that crisscross in back, which, at the end of the day, prevent an aching neck. But the commercially made shop aprons, such as those sold by Duluth Trading Company® (800-505-8888) work well as long as you don't overload them. What you decide to carry around in your apron is ultimately an individual decision, but once you start wearing one, I think you'll find it a real timesaver.

STEVE LATTA is an instructor at the Thaddeus Stevens College of Technology in Lancaster, Pennsylvania.

SAFETY GLASSES Choose eyewear that offers plenty of protection to the sides as well as the front.

ADJUSTABLE BEVEL? The Starrett #47 is compact and precise.

6-IN. RULER Choose one with 1⁄64-in. graduations.

LUMBER CRAYONS Use multiple colors to label stock for multiple runs.

FINGER PADS These are great at protecting your fingers from heat buildup when using a card scraper.

LAMINATE SCRAPS

4-IN. PRECISION DOUBLE SQUARE Shown is the Starrett No. 4R.

COUNTERSINK Models that use an Allen wrench to adjust the depth of the drill bit are more versatile.

MAGNETIC BIT HOLDER WITH MULTIPLE TIPS Phillips #1 and #2, a #2 square drive, and a few slotted tips should cover most situations.

DRILL BITS Keep small bits on hand to drill pilot holes for hardware and jigs. A small tube makes a practical storage container.

STOP BLOCK This shopmade block is hinged, which allows it to swing out of the way when making the first cut to square an end.

C-CLAMP Use this small one primarily for clamping a stop block to a fence.

TAPE MEASURE Choose a good-quality 12-ft. or 16-ft. measure with a ¾-in.-wide blade.

PARAFFIN WAX A small chunk is good for lubricating such things as screw threads and miter-gauge slots.

X-ACTO KNIFE Cover with the cap when returning the knife to your apron.

Not Your Father's Pegboard

BY HANK GILPIN

The first thing people notice when they visit my shop is the tool rack. Not the wood scattered and stacked everywhere, not the furniture under construction, not the big old machines. Nope, they always walk over to the wall of open tool and clamp storage and say, "Wow, your shop is so organized."

I'm never sure if the shop's neatness is a letdown or a pleasant surprise. But it doesn't really matter. I didn't build my tool rack for display. I am neat by nature and by need fairly organized. We do a lot of hand-work at my shop, and because I always have at least one other person working with me, I wanted a rack that would put the full array of hand tools within arm's length of two benches.

The wall's layout is simple and practical. Each of the primary tools—every plane, chisel, file, measuring device, and saw—has a spot to sit in and can be taken out with-out moving anything else. Blades stay sharp, squares stay true, and saws stay straight. The slanted shelves for the planes and chisels make the tools easy to locate and grab. A strip of wood tacked along the lower edge of these shelves keeps the tools from sliding off, and 5/16-in.-sq. strips between the tools keep them spaced properly.

ORGANIZATION OUT IN THE OPEN. It's easier to stay organized when tool storage is close at hand and unobstructed. The convenience of the author's simple system keeps tools from piling up on the bench.

The shallow shelves above the plane and chisel racks hold sanding blocks, mallets, drills, and the less frequently used planes and scrapers. At the bottom of the rack is hanging storage for clamps and shelving for the myriad blocks, wedges, battens, and pads used with the clamps.

I didn't rush into the rack's design. I thought about my work habits and sketched out a number of alternative arrangements. But I built the entire project in one day. I used construction-grade plywood and nailed and glued it together.

I don't think I could come up with a simpler, easier-to-use solution. After 24 years of use, it serves the shop well.

HANK GILPIN makes custom furniture in Lincoln, Rhode Island.

Credits

Index